Elephants
& Other Land Giants

A TIME-LIFE TELEVISION BOOK

Produced in Association with Vineyard Books, Inc.

Editor: Eleanor Graves
Senior Consultant: Lucille Ogle
Text Editor: Milton Orshefsky
   Associate Text Editor: Bonnie Johnson
   Authors: Prue and John Napier, Tony Chiu, Thomas A. Dozier, Ivan Kaye
   Assistant Editors: Harold C. Field, Regina Grant Hersey
   Literary Research: Ellen Schachter
   Text Research: M. Caputineanu-Minden, Thomas Fitzharris
   Copy Editors: Peter Ainslie, Robert J. Myer
Picture Editor: Richard O. Pollard
   Picture Research: Judith Greene
   Permissions: Celia Waters
Book Designer and Art Director: Jos. Trautwein
   Assistant Art Director: David Russell
Production Coordinator: Jane L. Quinson

WILD, WILD WORLD OF ANIMALS
TELEVISION PROGRAM
Producers: Jonathan Donald and Lothar Wolff
This Time-Life Television Book is published by Time-Life Films, Inc.
Bruce L. Paisner, *President*
J. Nicoll Durrie, *Business Manager*

THE CONSULTANTS

WILLIAM G. CONWAY, General Director of the New York Zoological Society, is an internationally known zoologist with a special interest in wildlife conservation. He is on the boards of a number of scientific and conservation organizations, including the U. S. Appeal of the World Wildlife Fund and the Cornell Laboratory of Ornithology. He is a past president of the American Association of Zoological Parks and Aquariums.

DR. JAMES W. WADDICK, Curator of Education of the New York Zoological Society, is a herpetologist specializing in amphibians. He has written for many scientific journals and has participated in expeditions to Mexico, Central America, and Ecuador. He is a member of the American Society of Ichthyologists and Herpetologists, a Fellow of the American Association of Zoological Parks and Aquariums, and a member of its Public Education Committee.

JAMES G. DOHERTY, as Curator of Mammals for the New York Zoological Society, supervises the mammal collection of approximately 1,000 specimens at the Society's Zoological Park in the Bronx, New York. He is the author of many articles on the natural history, captive breeding, and management of mammals. He is a member of the American Association of Mammalogists and a Fellow of the American Association of Zoological Parks and Aquariums.

DR. DONALD BRUNING, Curator of Ornithology of the New York Zoological Society and adjunct associate professor of zoology at Fordham University, has written numerous articles on birds. He was a delegate to the International Ornithological Congress and to the International Committee for Bird Preservation in Canberra, Australia, in 1974. He has done extensive research on rheas in Argentina.

MARK MACNAMARA is Assistant Curator of Mammals at the New York Zoological Society.

Wild, Wild World of Animals

Elephants
& Other Land Giants

Based on the television series
Wild, Wild World of Animals

Published by

TIME-LIFE FILMS

Contents

Introduction by Prue and John Napier

THERE ARE SEVERAL KINDS OF GIANTS in the animal kingdom. One is the individual giant that is simply a freak. A classic example is the Monster Pig, nine feet long, 2,800 pounds, which caused a sensation in London in 1867. A second kind is a species that is called giant only because it is larger than the size considered normal by the person describing it. Early Victorian voyagers to the tropics, for example, were impressed by "giant" spiders as big as dinner plates, by "giant" snails and by "giant" squirrels; the python was a "giant" to people accustomed to nothing larger than an adder or a grass snake.

Another kind of giant, the most spectacular of all, consists of animals—such as the elephant, the rhinoceros, the giraffe and others—that are large in an absolute sense. They tower over puny man, striking awe in his breast by their strangeness and unfamiliarity as well as by their huge size. It is with this last group of giants that this book is concerned.

Increase in absolute size is one of the most widespread trends in animal evolution. It has affected all classes. There are giant invertebrates (like the giant squids), giant mammals (whales), and there have been giant reptiles (dinosaurs). There is undoubtedly an evolutionary advantage in being *slightly* larger than one's contemporaries, so it is inevitable that natural selection, the mechanism by which evolution takes place, should tend to favor the larger members of an animal population and reject the smaller. In this way each new generation, the offspring of larger animals, will carry the genetic material for a larger size that will thus, gradually, be assimilated into the species. We can see the results of this natural selection, through time, in a series of closely related fossil forms such as those of the horse. The modern horse is a "giant" compared with its ancestor, the tiny, terrier-size *Hyracotherium*, the dawn horse of 60 million years ago. And modern man dwarfs his remote ancestors.

Mankind has grown up with a profound respect for bigness. We admire high mountains, large buildings, giant animals and tall men simply because they are big. Parents of babies slightly larger than average feel an irrational satisfaction, as though they had done something particularly clever in producing such a paragon. Throughout its young life a "tall-for-its-age" child is a source of pride to its parents until the son reaches six feet six inches and demands a king-size bed, or the daughter attains six feet and towers over most of her boyfriends. Clearly, large size has drawbacks as well as advantages.

In animals the advantages of size are obvious. Generally speaking, large animals are less likely to be attacked by predators. They can often move farther and faster than small animals. They have larger brains, with better memories, and so are generally more intelligent. They also live longer. An elephant's life-span is about 60 years, roughly the same as a man's.

The main disadvantage giant animals have is that they need enormous amounts of food to keep them alive. On the whole, large animals eat bulk foods that are abundant, such as grasses and leaves, rather than meat or insects. Elephants, hippos, rhinos, giraffes and even gorillas are all herbivores—

8

Brachiosaurus was the largest land animal that ever lived.

grazers or browsers on the exuberant vegetation of the African forests and savannas. This is one of the reasons why the largest land mammals are found in the tropics, where food is plentiful all year round.

Another problem that affects large mammals is temperature control. Unlike cold-blooded reptiles and fish, mammals maintain their body temperatures at a certain level, with only slight daily variations. The temperatures of the largest and smallest mammals are surprisingly similar. A man's temperature is 98.6° F., an elephant's 97.1° F. and a mouse's 97.7° F. But maintaining this temperature involves regulating heat gain and heat loss very precisely, and here the size of the animal is crucial.

Mammals generate heat by burning up food as fuel to power the body's activities, so the amount of heat gain is in proportion to body volume. They lose heat by radiation through the skin, so the amount of heat loss depends on the surface area of the body. This sounds perfectly simple until it is realized that, on the "potato principle," the relationship between volume and surface area alters with actual size. Anyone who has ever peeled potatoes knows that small potatoes produce much more peel than an equivalent amount of large potatoes. The reason becomes clear when a large potato is cut into quarters: The four small potatoes that result have skin on *one* surface only.

Sticking with this analogy, let us take a roughly potato-shaped animal as an example. The four-ton hippopotamus generates heat in proportion to its vast bulk but can lose it only through its skin, a relatively small area of surface. Its

VOLUME　　　　　　　**AREA**

A

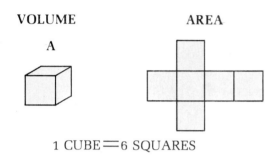

1 CUBE = 6 SQUARES

B

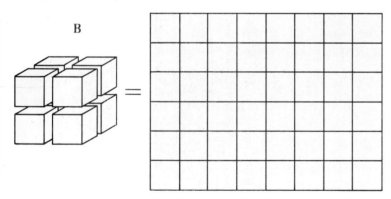

8 CUBES = 48 SQUARES

C

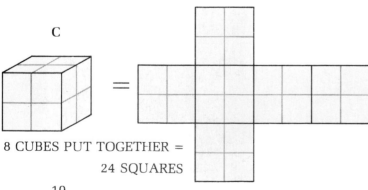

8 CUBES PUT TOGETHER =
24 SQUARES

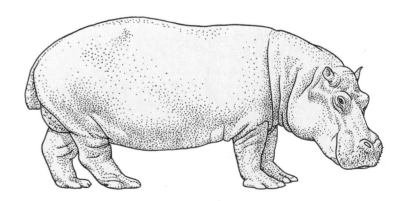

whole way of life is concentrated on keeping cool. Hippos, living under the blazing African sun, take to the water during the day and emerge only in the cool of the night. On the other hand, the smallest mammal, the pygmy shrew, weighing one eighth of an ounce, generates only minute amounts of heat, which it radiates very quickly through its relatively large surface area. Its thermo-regulating problems are completely different; it has to eat almost incessantly just to keep warm.

Elephants too have difficulties keeping cool, but their great flapping ears provide extra skin surface for heat loss. The temperature of the blood going into an elephant's ear can be as much as 16° F. higher than the blood leaving the ear—evidence for an impressive cooling mechanism.

The giraffe has no particular difficulties with heat loss, but its long neck poses a unique circulation problem: supplying blood to the brain, which may be 10 feet above the heart. To compensate for the pull of gravity, the giraffe has a higher blood pressure than any other animal—an average of 260/160 as compared to 120/80 in man, for example. And to compensate for this high pressure inside the walls of the blood vessels, the walls themselves are extremely thick and elastic. It is thought that the cerebrospinal fluid surrounding the brain and spinal cord may provide external pressure on the vessels to help keep them from bursting.

The giraffe moves with elegance and grace. But most large mammals cannot accelerate, change direction quickly or stop suddenly. The heavier the animal, the more effort is needed to get it under way, and the more powerful must be the braking system to bring it to a halt. A rhinoceros, for example, accelerates slowly, but once it is charging, it takes a lot of stopping. Nevertheless, it is a great deal more agile than it looks.

Like mammals, birds too have problems with giantism. Size, shape and, above all, weight are even more important in the air than on the ground. The wing area providing the "lift" that enables creatures to fly and soar is very precisely related to their weight, whether it is a hummingbird weighing less than a dime or a mute swan, which, at 30 pounds, is one of the heaviest birds ever to fly. Birds heavier than that, such as the ostrich, the emu, the rhea and the cassowary, discussed in this book, have grown so large that they simply can no longer get off the ground.

How they got that way is a long, evolutionary story. The earliest known bird, the feathered *Archaeopteryx*, took to the air some 150 million years ago in the Jurassic period. At the end of the Cretaceous period, 70 million years ago, all the dinosaurs died out and birds and little rat-sized mammals began to take over the strange, empty world the giant reptiles had left behind. At that time some birds found that they no longer needed to fly to escape predators, and they became ground-living. Gradually they increased in size, developing stout legs and large feet to support their weight. Their wings became obsolete or changed in function. The elephant bird of Madagascar had tiny wings, while in the moa of New Zealand the whole of the wing structure was absent.

Ranged against Brachiosaurus, at 55 tons the biggest land animal ever to exist, the land giants of today look puny. Each is shown with a smaller member of its family thought to resemble, if not actually be, an ancestor. Protosuchus, a primitive crocodile, lived about 170 million years ago and, except for its longer legs, was similar in structure and habits to the crocodile of today. Moeritherium, a pig-sized member of the elephant family, lived 35 million years ago in the swamps of present-day Egypt. Archaeopteryx, the first known bird, lived 180 million years ago and was probably not much of a flyer. Paleotragus, an early giraffe, looked much like the present-day okapi. The origin of the hippopotamus is obscure, but one early member of its family, Bothriodon, was also pig-sized and had certain other affinities to pigs that the swinelike hippo shares. Hyrachus, a rhinoceros of the Eocene epoch, was about the size of a large dog. Paraceratherium, a gentle browser and an extinct Asiatic cousin of today's rhino, was the largest land mammal ever to exist. The turtle family tree is another question mark, but the first true turtle, Proganochelys, was not much smaller than the Galápagos giant of today.

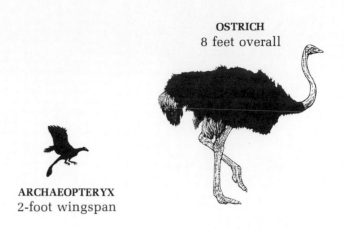

OSTRICH
8 feet overall

ARCHAEOPTERYX
2-foot wingspan

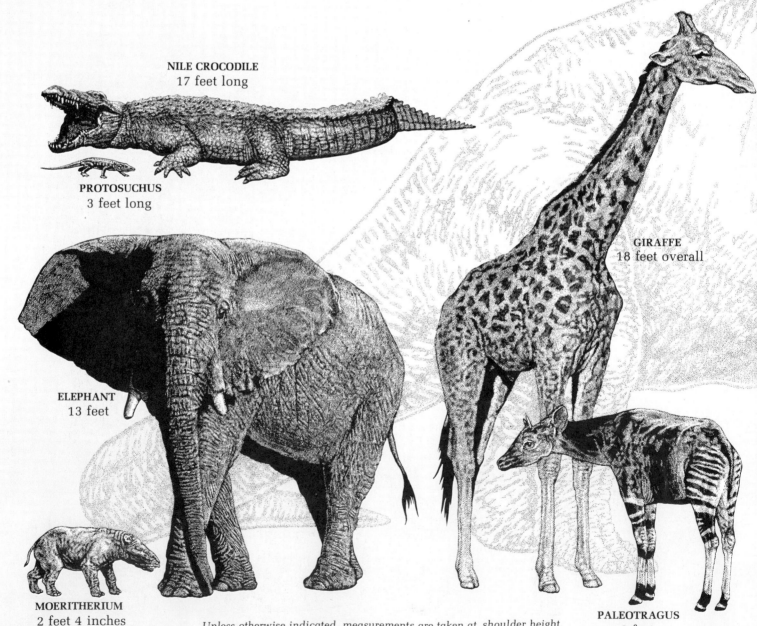

NILE CROCODILE
17 feet long

PROTOSUCHUS
3 feet long

GIRAFFE
18 feet overall

ELEPHANT
13 feet

MOERITHERIUM
2 feet 4 inches

PALEOTRAGUS
6 feet

Unless otherwise indicated, measurements are taken at shoulder height.

BRACHIOSAURUS
80 feet long

PROGANOCHELYS
4 feet long

HIPPOPOTAMUS
5 feet

GALÁPAGOS TORTOISE
5 feet long

BOTHRIODON
2½ feet

PARACERATHERIUM
18 feet

RHINOCEROS
5½ feet

HYRACHUS
3½ feet

13

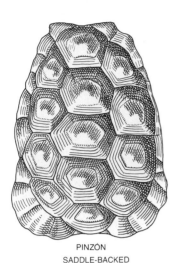

PINZÓN
SADDLE-BACKED

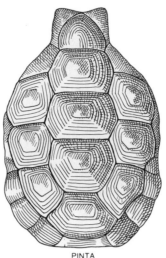

PINTA
SADDLE-BACKED

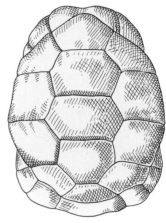

ISABELA
DOME-SHAPED

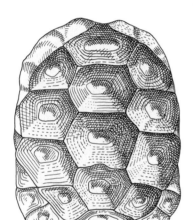

SANTA CRUZ
DOME-SHAPED

The distinctive shapes and patterns of the shells of four of the 11 surviving subspecies of Galápagos tortoises are shown above. In addition to the striking differences in design that are often used in identifying each subspecies, these tortoises' shells show two further variations. The tortoises that live in areas with lush ground vegetation, such as those from the islands of Santa Cruz and Isabela, have dome-shaped shells. Those that have to stretch for their food, for example the subspecies from Pinzón and Pinta, have evolved shells with raised front portions, called saddle-backed shells, that allow the animals' necks a longer reach.

These two birds vie for the record as the largest bird of all time. The elephant bird stood 10 feet tall and weighed up to 1,000 pounds, while the moa, at 12 to 13 feet, is thought to have weighed about 500 pounds.

Both the moa and the elephant bird have become extinct within historical times. Both lived on islands that had no large carnivores to prey on them, and there they flourished until man, the most ruthless carnivore of all, invaded their sanctuaries. The classic example of extinction caused by man is the dodo from the island of Mauritius. Stolid, cumbersome and not very bright, it was defenseless in the face of man and all his camp followers—dogs, cats and rats—and has become the very symbol of extinction.

An island sometimes provides a sanctuary for its inhabitants and thus can be a forcing ground for evolution. Charles Darwin, visiting the Galápagos Islands in 1835, found giant tortoises with differently shaped shells on each of the 10 main islands. The isolation and the lack of both predators and competitors had allowed each island population to develop its own peculiar shell-type. At 500 to 600 pounds, they are all much larger than their relatives in South America, from which their progenitor—probably an egg-bearing female—must have journeyed, floating on a raft of driftwood. Since Darwin's day, many of the 15 original forms have become extinct, mainly through the ravages of man and the mammals he introduced, particularly pigs, goats and dogs, which have destroyed much of the unique vegetation—the tortoises' staple food—as well as young tortoises and their nests.

The Komodo dragon, the giant lizard named for the island of Komodo in Indonesia, also lacks both predators and competitors, but it has to be protected by law to save it from extermination by the local farmers.

Giantism is frequently the end of the line; giant animals usually do not leave small-sized descendants. The most common thing that happens to a giant breed is that it becomes extinct, because it is more difficult for giants to adapt to changing environments. The Pleistocene epoch, the geological time period that began two million years ago and lasted until about 10,000 years ago, produced a series of outsize forms of certain familiar animals that today are not regarded as giants in any sense— baboons, sheep, oxen and pigs. All these have been discovered in fossils at Olduvai Gorge, Tanzania. It is true that we have baboons and sheep and all the rest still with us, but these animals are not, strictly speaking, descendants of the giant Pleistocene species, which disappeared from the fossil record and left no direct descendants. Present-day sheep and Pleistocene sheep spring from a common ancestor, but they are probably related as cousins are related rather than as father and son.

Giant animals tend to carry within themselves the seeds of their own destruction. When conditions are ideal and food is plentiful they can survive, but when competition from other animals gets too fierce (as might well have happened during the Pleistocene ice ages or the African pluvials, or rainy periods) their demands in terms of food supply cannot be met, and they die out. Clearly, too, there must be an upper limit to the size of the body that limbs can support without loss of mobility. This threshold for land animals was probably reached by the extinct giants of the age of reptiles, the dinosaurs.

The dinosaurs, or "terrible lizards," were not all giants. They ranged from a few feet to 80 feet in length and flourished over a period of some 130 million years, reaching their peak during the Cretaceous period—between 135 and 70 million years ago. Both plant-eating and flesh-eating forms coexisted, in roughly the same proportions as herbivores and carnivores occur today among the mammals. The herbivorous dinosaurs browsed on the plants of the tropical forests that covered much of the land surface of the earth at that time. The biggest of them, the 80-foot, 55-ton *Brachiosaurus* and the *Diplodocus*, lived submerged up to their long necks in lakes and swamps, thus reducing the effects of gravity. They were preyed upon by the truly frightful *Tyrannosaurus rex*, 40 feet long and 20 feet high, its huge jaws embellished with dozens of bladelike teeth. We know tantalizingly little of their way of life and still less about why, at the end of the Cretaceous period, they suddenly became extinct—not only the giants but the small ones as well.

If the remaining land giants described in this book become extinct in the wild, man will certainly have had a good deal to do with it. It is the tragedy of man that he cannot leave anything alone, that he always has to interfere. His ignorant bumbling around the globe—whether in the name of exploration or just plain greed—has left a wake of disaster. Island faunas have been particularly badly affected, but even the bison, roaming the vast American prairies, barely escaped extinction. Today, everywhere, wildlife is in retreat before man's technological advance. Paradoxically, it is the largest animals that are the most vulnerable.

A world without giants and monsters would be a poorer place. It is not just a coincidence that, as large animals dwindle in numbers and become less frightening through familiarity, man creates his own monsters and giants to replace them. The Abominable Snowman of the Himalayas, the Sasquatch of North America and the Loch Ness Monster of the Scottish Highlands may be only figments of human imagination, but they fill a real gap in our culture.

15

African Elephants

There are few sights in this world more immediately guaranteed to stop the heart than that of an adult African elephant when it is surprised or threatened. The flapping ears, resembling freehand maps of Africa, may measure six feet from top to bottom. Extended in fear or anger, their total spread can be greater than the animal's height, some 10 to 20 feet. The nervously tensing trunk may be seven feet long; the forelegs, churning dust, look like structural columns. The whole impression is of sheer, powerful mass.

Of all mammals that have survived since the end of the last Ice Age, only whales are larger than elephants. The largest elephant killed in modern times stood more than 13 feet high at the shoulders and weighed almost 12 tons. Although many kinds of elephants existed in past eras, today there are only two—the African and the Asiatic. The Asiatic will be discussed on pages 50 through 63.

Next to its size, the most arresting feature of any elephant is its trunk. To support its massive head the animal has a muscular neck, which is too short to allow its mouth to reach the ground. As compensation, the elephant's snout and upper lips have evolved into a wondrous appendage three feet in circumference at the base, which serves as combination nose, hand, tool, food-and-water gatherer and auxiliary arm. When the wind is right the trunk can detect scents as far away as two miles. It tests unfamiliar terrain, touching each spot before the elephant moves. Equipped with an estimated 40,000 muscles, it can be a formidable weapon. But it is in obtaining food and water that it demonstrates its real versatility. It is sensitive and agile enough to pick up a single leaf or berry, and it can also suck up as much as a gallon and a half of water at a time.

Because the trunk is so essential to its survival, an elephant sensing danger will reflexively protect it by curling it inward into a tight spiral close to its body. A severe injury to its trunk can be tantamount to death by starvation. Even with a damaged trunk, however, elephants have shown themselves remarkably adaptable. Some feed only on reeds in the water; others kneel or tilt forward with one knee bent to browse on bushes. One case has even been reported of an elephant dragging grass to itself with one foot, working it up onto a tusk and then using the undamaged upper part of the trunk to push the food into its mouth.

Left undisturbed, the African ele-phant has a life expectancy, similar to man's, of 60 years or more. It is well equipped by nature to defend itself. In addition to being large and strong, it can attain speeds up to 20 to 25 miles per hour over short distances. When a threat appears, an elephant family forms a protective defense circle. Naturalist Iain Douglas-Hamilton reports, for example, that once when he shot an elephant calf with a tranquilizing dart in order to attach a radio tracking device, a total of 67 elephants quickly massed protectively around the fallen animal and prevented Douglas-Hamilton from continuing with his experiment.

But the elephant has not been left undisturbed. And its defenses have been of little value when arrayed against the devices of man, who since the days of Egypt's pharaohs has prized the elephant's tusks. Even before the turn of the century elephants had been eliminated from many parts of Africa and were heading steadily toward extinction. A strong demand for ivory from manufacturers of billiard balls and piano keys coincided with the spread of powerful rifles, and the result was carnage. Some naturalists estimate that in the early 1900s as many as 100,000 elephants were slaughtered each year. Most of the commercial pressure for ivory decreased in the 1940s with the appearance of plastics, only to revive in recent years, particularly in the Far East. There ivory is thought, like gold and precious gems, to provide insurance against weak currencies. And the developing countries of the African continent have been taming more and more land—and pushing the remaining elephants into game parks and preserves, some of which are so crowded that rangers must periodically kill some animals so that the rest may survive.

The African elephant is still not on the official endangered-species list, partly because of the overcrowding in the preserves and partly because nobody really has the remotest idea how many there are left. Most African countries now have antipoaching laws, but enforcement is spotty at best. In Kenya, for example, some 10,000 to 20,000 elephants are being killed every year. "It is difficult to get exact figures," says Douglas-Hamilton, "but it appears that elephants are being killed faster than they can reproduce themselves."

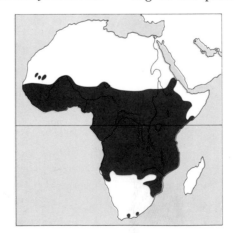

Elephants are dispersed over Africa from the southern rim of the Sahara to the forests of southern Africa.

Family Bonds

Elephants are sociable animals. The basic unit in their social organization is the tightly knit, affectionate family. Composed of several cows and their offspring, the family ranges in age from newborn babes to grandmothers. The young calves play constantly (below) under the protective eyes of the cows. Individual families maintain loose but regular contact with other kinship groups in the area. A gathering of families becomes a herd (right), whose size depends largely on the availability of food and water. If forage is plentiful, the herd is likely to be large; if scarce, not only is the herd smaller but individual families may fragment into even smaller groups.

Elephant society is completely matriarchal. The system works because of the strong bonds between the oldest cow and her female descendants. When young bulls reach the age of puberty at about 12, they are expelled from the family by adult cows to go off on their own or with other bulls. Bulls do not establish permanent relationships with family or kinship groups. They bear no responsibility for raising the young and probably don't know their own offspring. Their only function is the continuation of the species.

Against the magnificent backdrop of Mount Kilimanjaro in Tanzania, two bull elephants spar, trunk to trunk. This kind of play-fighting, indulged in throughout an elephant's life, is seldom serious. It seems to have two main functions: to learn combat techniques and maneuvers in case the elephants are ever called on to do serious fighting and to provide young animals with a way of testing and developing their strength.

20

A Touching Society

In amiable social situations elephants use trunks the way people use hands—for greeting, caressing or otherwise giving reassurance. A mother elephant lays her trunk soothingly on the forehead of her sick baby. A young elephant will greet an older, larger stranger by putting its trunk in the stranger's mouth. Members of the immediate family always seem to be touching each other affectionately (right). And in play-fighting, adult bulls, shown above alongside Lake Manyara in Tanzania, fence and spar with their trunks rather than their tusks, which could inflict real damage.

A Proper Start

Elephants do not engage in the elaborate courting rituals of some animals, but they will occasionally intertwine trunks. (In the picture above, the male is on the right.) If all goes well, 22 months after copulation a baby is born, weighing in at about 260 pounds and standing almost three feet high. It sometimes has trouble finding its food supply and settles for sucking its trunk (left). Once it has found its mother's teats it gobbles down about two and one half gallons of milk a day, feeding at frequent intervals. Calves are permitted to nurse until they are five or six years old, when their tusks become troublesome to their mothers.

Even a baby elephant, either instinctively or in imitation of its elders, indulges in threat-display (left) at the approach of an intruder. But it is much more fun romping with the other calves—in sex-play (below) or mock fights. The carefree fun goes on for a dozen years, until the age of puberty. Then the males are driven from the family, and the females are ready to take on the responsibilities of babies of their own.

A Long Happy Life

An elephant's potential life-span is about 60 years. In its first five years it doubles its weight and height. By age 30 an average elephant is almost fully grown—some nine to 12 feet at the shoulder. An African elephant's tusks never stop growing. It has been calculated that if the tusks survived without damage throughout the animal's life, they would measure 16 feet in the female and 20 feet in the bull. But long before death an elephant's tusks are broken (opposite), chipped and worn smooth by life's vicissitudes.

This aged bull elephant called Ahmed outlived all his contemporaries. He was protected in his later years from poachers by game wardens of the Marsabit National Preserve in Kenya, and he became a favorite with tourists and photographers. Although he had the largest tusks of any elephant in Kenya, it wasn't until his death in 1974, at the age of 55, that they could be weighed. It was then discovered that the massive but broken and scarred incisors weighed only 296 pounds—surprisingly little when compared to the 440½ pounds of the heaviest pair ever recorded.

Elephantine Conclave

A herd of elephants mills about on a grassy savanna. Cut off from their old migration routes because of man's usurpation of Africa's land, some elephants still gather during the seasons when once they began their journeys to new feeding places. Below, a typical small family. made up of a matriarch and her charges, ambles through a forest after having completed its morning ablutions.

The Elephant's Child
by Rudyard Kipling

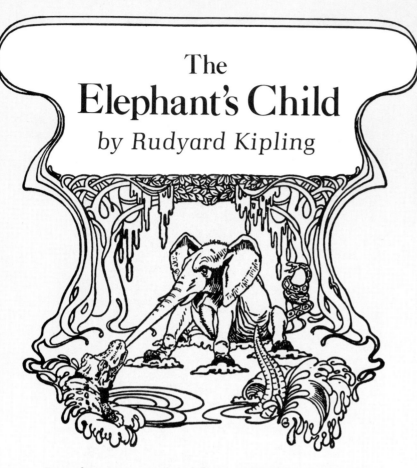

Even the youngest reader of Rudyard Kipling's Just So Stories *knows that animals do not behave the way they do in these tales, but for generations the stories have been read for their charming fantasy. The story that follows, "The Elephant's Child," describes how the African elephant got its trunk. It is illustrated here with Kipling's original drawings.*

In the high and Far-Off Times the Elephant, O Best Beloved, had no trunk. He had only a blackish, bulgy nose, as big as a boot, that he could wriggle about from side to side; but he couldn't pick up things with it. But there was one Elephant—a new Elephant—an Elephant's Child—who was full of 'satiable curtiosity, and that means he asked ever so many questions. And he lived in Africa, and he filled all Africa with his 'satiable curtiosities. He asked his tall aunt, the Ostrich, why her tail-feathers grew just so, and his tall aunt the Ostrich spanked him with her hard, hard claw. He asked his tall uncle, the Giraffe, what made his skin spotty, and his tall

uncle, the Giraffe, spanked him with his hard, hard hoof. And still he was full of 'satiable curtiosity! He asked his broad aunt, the Hippopotamus, why her eyes were red, and his broad aunt, the Hippopotamus, spanked him with her broad, broad hoof; and he asked his hairy uncle, the Baboon, why melons tasted just so, and his hairy uncle, the Baboon, spanked him with his hairy, hairy paw. And *still* he was full of 'satiable curtiosity! He asked questions about everything that he saw, or heard, or felt, or smelt, or touched, and all his uncles and his aunts spanked him. And still he was full of 'satiable curtiosity!

One fine morning in the middle of the Precession of the Equinoxes this 'satiable Elephant's Child asked a new fine question that he had never asked before. He asked, 'What does the Crocodile have for dinner?' Then everybody said, 'Hush!' in a loud and dretful tone, and they spanked him immediately and directly, without stopping, for a long time.

By and by, when that was finished, he came upon Kolokolo Bird sitting in the middle of a wait-a-bit thorn-bush, and he said, 'My father has spanked me, and my mother has spanked me; all my aunts and uncles have spanked me for my 'satiable curtiosity; and *still* I want to know what the Crocodile has for dinner!'

Then Kolokolo Bird said, with a mournful cry, 'Go to the banks of the great grey-green, greasy Limpopo River, all set about with fever-trees and find out.'

That very next morning, when there was nothing left of the Equinoxes because the Precession had preceded according to precedent, this 'satiable Elephant's Child took a hundred pounds of bananas (the little short red kind), and a hundred pounds of sugar-cane (the long purple kind), and seventeen melons (the greeny-crackly kind), and said to all his dear families, 'Good-bye. I am going to the great grey-green, greasy Limpopo River, all set about with fever-trees, to find out what the Crocodile has for dinner. And they all spanked him once more for luck, though he asked them most politely to stop.

Then he went away, a little warm, but not at all astonished, eating melons, and throwing the rind about, because he could not pick it up.

He went from Graham's Town to Kimberley, and from Kimberley to Khama's Country, and from Khama's Country he went east by north, eating melons all the time, till at last he came to the banks of the great grey-green, greasy Limpopo River, all set about with fever-trees, precisely as Kolokolo Bird had said.

Now you must know and understand, O Best Beloved, that till that very week, and day, and hour, and minute, this 'satiable Elephant's Child had never seen a Crocodile, and did not know what one was like. It was all his 'satiable curtiosity.

The first thing that he found was a Bi-Coloured-Python-Rock-Snake curled round a rock.

''Scuse me,' said the Elephant's Child most politely, 'but have you seen such a thing as a Crocodile in these promiscuous parts?'

'Have I seen a Crocodile?' said the Bi-Coloured-Python-Rock-Snake, in a voice of dretful scorn. 'What will you ask me next?'

''Scuse me,' said the Elephant's Child, 'but could you kindly tell me what he has for dinner?'

Then the Bi-Coloured-Python-Rock-Snake uncoiled himself very quickly from the rock, and spanked the Elephant's Child with his scalesome, flailsome tail.

'That is odd,' said the Elephant's Child, 'because my father and my mother, and my uncle and my aunt, not to mention my other aunt, the Hippopotamus, and my other uncle, the Baboon, have all spanked me for my 'satiable curtiosity—and I suppose this is the same thing.'

So he said good-bye very politely to the Bi-Coloured-Python-Rock-Snake, and helped to coil him up on the rock again, and went on, a little warm, but not at all astonished, eating melons, and throwing the rind about, because he could not pick it up, till he trod on what he

29

thought was a log of wood at the very edge of the great grey-green, greasy Limpopo River, all set about with fever-trees.

But it was really the Crocodile, O Best Beloved, and the Crocodile winked one eye—like this!

''Scuse me,' said the Elephant's Child most politely, 'but do you happen to have seen a Crocodile in these promiscuous parts?'

Then the Crocodile winked the other eye, and lifted half his tail out of the mud; and the Elephant's Child stepped back most politely, because he did not wish to be spanked again.

'Come hither, Little One,' said the Crocodile. 'Why do you ask such things?'

''Scuse me,' said the Elephant's Child most politely, 'but my father has spanked me, my mother has spanked me, not to mention my tall aunt, the Ostrich, and my tall uncle, the Giraffe, who can kick ever so hard, as well as my broad aunt, the Hippopotamus, and my hairy uncle, the Baboon, and including the Bi-Coloured-Python-Rock-Snake, with the scalesome, flailsome tail, just up the bank, who spanks harder than any of them; and *so*, if it's quite all the same to you, I don't want to be spanked any more.'

'Come hither, Little One,' said the Crocodile, 'for I am the Crocodile,' and he wept crocodile-tears to show it was quite true.

Then the Elephant's Child grew all breathless, and panted, and kneeled down on the bank and said, 'You are the very person I have been looking for all these long days. Will you please tell me what you have for dinner?'

'Come hither, Little One,' said the Crocodile, 'and I'll whisper.'

Then the Elephant's Child put his head down close to the Crocodile's musky, tusky mouth, and the Crocodile caught him by his little nose, which up to that very week, day, hour, and minute, had been no bigger than a boot, though much more useful.

'I think,' said the Crocodile—and he said it between his teeth, like this— 'I think to-day I will begin with Elephant's Child!'

At this, O Best Beloved, the Elephant's Child was much annoyed, and he said, speaking through his nose, like this, 'Led go! You are hurtig be!'

Then the Bi-Coloured-Python-Rock-Snake scuffled down from the bank and said, 'My young friend, if you do not now, immediately and instantly, pull as hard as ever you can, it is my opinion that your acquaintance in the large-pattern leather ulster' (and by this he meant the Crocodile) 'will jerk you into yonder limpid stream before you can say Jack Robinson.'

This is the way Bi-Coloured-Python-Rock-Snakes always talk.

Then the Elephant's Child sat back on his little haunches, and pulled, and pulled, and pulled, and his nose began to stretch. And the Crocodile floundered into the water, making it all creamy with great sweeps of his tail, and *he* pulled, and pulled, and pulled.

And the Elephant's Child's nose kept on stretching; and the Elephant's Child spread all his little four legs and pulled, and pulled, and pulled, and his nose kept on stretching; and the Crocodile threshed his tail like an oar, and *he* pulled, and pulled, and pulled, and at each pull the Elephant's Child's nose grew longer and longer—and it hurt him hijjus!

Then the Elephant's Child felt his legs slipping, and he said through his nose, which was now nearly five feet long, 'This is too butch for be!'

Then the Bi-Coloured-Python-Rock-Snake came down from the bank, and knotted himself in a double-clove-hitch round the Elephant's Child's hind legs, and said, 'Rash and inexperienced traveller, we will now seriously devote ourselves to a little high tension, because if we do not, it is my impression that yonder self-propelling man-of-war with the armour-plated upper deck' (and by this, O Best Beloved, he meant the Crocodile), 'will permanently vitiate your future career.'

That is the way all Bi-Coloured-Python-Rock-Snakes always talk.

So he pulled, and the Elephant's Child pulled, and the Crocodile pulled; but the Elephant's Child and the Bi-Coloured-Python-Rock-Snake pulled hardest; and at last the Crocodile let go of the Elephant's Child's nose with a plop that you could hear all up and down the Limpopo.

Then the Elephant's Child sat down most hard and sudden; but first he was careful to say 'Thank you' to the Bi-Coloured-Python-Rock-Snake; and next he was kind to his poor pulled nose, and wrapped it all up in cool banana leaves, and hung it in the great grey-green, greasy Limpopo to cool.

'What are you doing that for?' said the Bi-Coloured-Python-Rock-Snake.

''Scuse me,' said the Elephant's Child, 'but my nose is badly out of shape, and I am waiting for it to shrink.'

'Then you will have to wait a long time,' said the Bi-Coloured-Python-Rock-Snake. 'Some people do not know what is good for them.'

The Elephant's Child sat there for three days waiting for his nose to shrink. But it never grew any shorter, and, besides, it made him squint. For, O Best Beloved, you will see and understand that the Crocodile had pulled it out into a really truly trunk same as all Elephants have to-day.

At the end of the third day a fly came and stung him on the shoulder, and before he knew what he was doing he lifted up his trunk and hit that fly dead with the end of it.

''Vantage number one!' said the Bi-Coloured-Python-Rock-Snake. 'You couldn't have done that with a mere-smear nose. Try and eat a little now.'

Before he thought what he was doing the Elephant's Child put out his trunk and plucked a large bundle of grass, dusted it clean against his fore-legs, and stuffed it into his own mouth.

' 'Vantage number two!' said the Bi-Coloured-Python-Rock-Snake. 'You couldn't have done that with a mere-smear nose. Don't you think the sun is very hot here?'

'It is,' said the Elephant's Child, and before he thought what he was doing he schlooped up a schloop of mud from the banks of the great grey-green, greasy Limpopo, and slapped it on his head, where it made a cool schloopy-sloshy mud-cap all trickly behind his ears.

''Vantage number three!' said the Bi-Coloured-Python-Rock-Snake. 'You couldn't have done that with a mere-smear nose. Now how do you feel about being

spanked again?'

''Scuse me,' said the Elephant's Child, 'but I should not like it at all.'

'How would you like to spank somebody?' said the Bi-Coloured-Python-Rock-Snake.

'I should like it very much indeed,' said the Elephant's Child.

'Well,' said the Bi-Coloured-Python-Rock-Snake, 'you will find that new nose of yours very useful to spank people with.'

'Thank you,' said the Elephant's Child, 'I'll remember that; and now I think I'll go home to all my dear families and try.'

31

An elephant nibbles at the foliage of a tall acacia tree (left), making good use of its great height and remarkably dexterous trunk. Since acacia seeds have a better chance of germinating if they pass through an animal, this feeding habit of the elephant gains it some good marks. On the other hand, elephants have been accused of destroying whole forests to satisfy their ravenous appetites.

A Ruinous Appetite

Feeding is an elephant's principal activity. Since it digests only 40 percent of its food, an adult must spend 16 hours a day searching for and munching the 500 pounds it needs to fuel its enormous body. Elephants eat mostly grass, but despite their need for quantity, they have notions about quality as well and are especially fond of such things as wild celery, black plums, desert dates and wild raspberries. In the Lake Manyara area in Tanzania, where food is plentiful, elephants are known to dine off at least 134 of the 630 plant species.

An elephant's unique physical equipment is of great help in foraging. In lean times its tusks gouge the bark from baobab trees so that its trunk can pick up the pieces (left). Then, using tusks, trunk, head and the strength of its body, it pushes over the gutted baobab (above) to get at the water in the tree's fibrous interior.

33

The devastation wrought by crowded elephants in their search for food is dramatic—a dead baobab tree (above), acres of ravished acacia trees (opposite)—and has touched off an ecological debate among naturalists. Some contend that unless elephant herds are vigorously culled, or thinned out, the elephants themselves will die out for lack of food, and so will other animals. Other naturalists argue against culling, claiming that not enough is yet known about the long-range effects of the elephants' destruction of trees and that it is preferable to allow nature to run its cyclical course: Elephants knock down trees, grasslands replace them; elephants decline in number; grazing animals take over the grassland; the land becomes unfit for anything but bushes and trees, and they eventually proliferate once more; the elephants return to a now ideal woodlands habitat. Cycles of this kind might take 100 years, but there is evidence that this is what is already happening in Kenya and Tanzania.

A tranquil lake in South-West Africa provides ample drinking water for the stately elephants at right, while the calf below must be satisfied with what little water remains in a well dug by its elders. The young elephant on the opposite page glistens contentedly in a water-lily pond deep enough for bathing as well as drinking.

A Way with Water

The rhythm of an elephant's day is set largely by its watering routine. An adult needs about 30 gallons of water a day. When water is abundant there is no problem. But during droughts elephants resort to an intriguing technique: digging wells. In a dried-up riverbed they scoop out holes with their forefeet until they reach water. After waiting patiently for the sand to settle, they drink in order of seniority—calves (left) last. Elephants spray water over their ears to stay cool. So vital is this to their survival that in extreme drought conditions elephants have been known to put their trunks deep inside their own throats, sucking out water with which to cool themselves.

The complicated process of skin care begins with a long, luxurious wallow in mud (left). While the mud helps cool the elephant, it also provides a sticky base for the cloud of sand and dust that the elephant then blows all over itself (opposite). The mudpack plus the powdered earth coats the hide (below), protecting it against the sun. It also provides a respite from fresh onslaughts of insects.

Rigorous Grooming

Good grooming is an essential ritual, for the elephant's thick skin is highly sensitive to heat, bruises and insect bites. One step in the process—the sand shower—gives elephants a temporary coloring of the country they inhabit. The elephants above are coated with the white dust of Etosha Park in South-West Africa. In other areas they may appear brown, ocher or even red. At the end of the grooming process they find a handy object to rub against—either a tree or a termite hill (left) The rubbing pulverizes the parasites that plague elephants.

The young bull on the left is no longer wanted in his family group, but he is extremely reluctant to leave. He has challenged a cow who tried to chase him away but was careful to place himself on higher ground, just out of range of the cow's tusks.

Out of My Way!

Fights between bull elephants (above) are probably rare because the hierarchy among bulls is established during adolescence, and each animal therefore knows when to give in and when to assert himself. Intimidation, when it does occur, is of the mildest sort; slight differences in the position of head, legs or trunk are enough. Bulls are good-natured animals and, in protected areas, lead a pleasant way of life: no enemies, no responsibilities. Even in unprotected areas they do not have to defend territories, as many other animals do. Bulls occasionally form groups that travel and feed together for several hours or days at a time, but these associations are fleeting. Nevertheless, a solitary bull is rarely found more than a mile away from another bull or family unit.

Among the Elephants

by Iain and Oria Douglas-Hamilton

In the mid-1960s a young Scottish zoologist, Iain Douglas-Hamilton, and his photographer wife, Oria, lived in Tanzania where they studied the ecology of elephant herds. Their daily observations of the elephants enabled them to recognize individuals, to follow families and track herds and thus to develop a new and compelling view of these animals.

The following passage from Among the Elephants *is Iain's eyewitness account of an elephant's death.*

To me the death of an elephant is one of the saddest sights in the world. The day I met Torone Sister Number Four unexpectedly in the Ndala woods she was an epitome of vigorous life, a powerful strident member of her species, the growth of scores of years had fused her skeleton and muscles into a marvellous organism, co-ordinated by a brain conditioned by decades of experience. Motivated, at that instant, in defence of her family, she bore down, like a mighty battleship going full speed ahead, upon Mhoja and me. Next second, separated only by a pin-point in time and the deadly passage of lead through living tissues, she was a collapsed mound of flesh, a colossal lifeless wreck, with a tiny hole in her head from which came a thin trickle of blood.

To a statistician the only significance of death is in its effects on population dynamics and the causes of death are

---

The sequence of pictures beginning on this page shows the death of a matriarch witnessed in 1970 in Serengeti National Park, Kenya, by ecologist Harvey Croze and photographer Horst Munzig. The sequence begins with the dying cow sinking to her haunches as members of the herd form a protective semicircle about her.

43

analysed for their relative importance. For human beings and for elephants death remains significant in the behaviour of the survivors. In life individuals of both species are tied by strong family bonds and frantic attempts may be made to save a sick or dying relative.

Many great zoologists including Charles Darwin have thought that animals possess strong emotions and I have little doubt that when one of their number dies and the bonds of a lifetime are severed, elephants have a similar feeling to the one we call grief. Unfortunately science as yet has no means of measuring or describing emotion even for human beings, let alone for animals.

It is perhaps not surprising that attempts to assist a dying elephant may continue long after it is dead. Mhoja and I searching for more elephant paths up to the Marang Forest one day heard the loud bawling of an elephant calf in distress about a hundred feet up the Endabash escarpment. It was coming from our left, so we cautiously worked our way across the face of the scarp until we were very close to the source of the noise. Peering through the foliage I could make out the head of a cow at a curious angle to the slope. Her eye was open but she didn't move. In front of me a tree jutted out, and by swinging up into its branches I was able to get a better view.

With a convulsion the cow heaved onto her side. One young bull remained beside her, trying repeatedly to lift her onto her feet. One by one, family units within the herd returned to the body as if to mourn.

44

The young elephants pressed forward (right), and one tried to rouse the dying cow by placing a foot on her back. Finally, the young bull attempted to mount her. "It almost seemed as if he had tried every behaviour he could think of, threatening, lifting, feeding," according to Croze, "and turned in desperation to sex."

Now I saw quite clearly a scene of great natural drama. The cow, an adult, was lying on her side down the slope; one of her hind feet was wedged between a boulder and a thick tree and she was hanging from it. Her head was bent backwards at an acute angle and she was stone dead. Next to her stood three calves of different sizes. The eldest was moaning quietly but every so often gave vent to a passionate bawl. The second just stood dumbly motionless, its head resting against its mother's body. The smallest calf, less than a year old, made forlorn attempts to suck from her breasts. Then the eldest knelt down and pushed its head and small tusks against the corpse, in a hopeless attempt to move it. I watched them for fifteen minutes repeating these patterns of behaviour until suddenly they caught my wind and wandered slowly away.

45

When the last spark of life faded away, the attendant herd trumpeted loudly and began grazing nervously nearby. As the day waned, the mourning elephants approached the body in turn, and then at dusk the herd slowly and reluctantly moved away.

On closer inspection I found that the cow was still warm and that no flies had settled on her, so the accident must have happened only a short time earlier. Trees which had stood in the path of her fall were broken and boulders dislodged. I back-tracked the path of her descent to a point about 400 feet up the slope where I found her last footprints. It appeared that she had stepped into a pig hole covered in vegetation, lost her balance and rolled out of control down the precipitous slopes. There were several cliffs and in places it looked as if she had bounced down them leaving the vegetation undamaged. The calves must have had some difficulty in finding her afterwards, for the nature of the terrain would have forced them to make a wide detour. It seemed that they were not aware that she was dead, although they must have known something was wrong. Perhaps they could not adjust immediately to the finality of her death.

Similar behaviour has been well authenticated elsewhere. Shortly after this incident Harvey Croze and a photographer friend of his witnessed the death of an old cow in the middle of her family unit in the Serengeti [picture sequence pages 42–47]. Her dying dragged out over an afternoon in that lovely rolling northern country, not far from where we had darted the young bull. Harvey first noticed her lagging behind the family unit; when she fell they all clustered around her, putting their trunks in her mouth, pushing against her and trying to raise her. The most prominent was an independent bull who happened to be with the cows and calves, and he at times kept the others at bay while he attempted alone to aid the dying elephant. She died there among her family, and they stayed with her for several hours longer. The bull in his frustration at failing to raise her, indulged in totally irrelevant behaviour. He mounted the dead cow as if he were attempting to copulate, before finally moving off with the others. One cow, presumably she had a particularly strong bond with the dead animal, stayed longer than the others, only withdrawing reluctantly at nightfall.

A more extreme attachment to a dead animal was witnessed by Bill Woodley, the Warden of the Aberdares National Park in Kenya, who told me he observed cows

47

and calves defending the body of a young female for three days after it had been shot, and even more bizarre is the account given by Rennie Bere in his book *The African Elephant* of a cow who refused to abandon the decomposing corpse of her new-born calf, and carried it round for days resting on her tusks. The only other animals I have heard of doing this are baboon mothers who may carry a dead baby for a week or more.

Such a responsiveness to inert bodies is of obvious value in saving a member of a group who has temporarily collapsed. The helpers may also later benefit from the sick animal's recovery when it resumes its role in the family unit's life. It may participate in the communal rearing and defence of the calves, or if it is the matriarch herself, may continue to lead in times of stress and benefit the family unit by drawing on her accumulated stores of experience. A zoologist brought up in the theory of natural selection must always try to explain such apparently altruistic behaviour in terms of the helper's own advantage, or in cases where one animal sacrifices itself to save another, such behaviour must statistically tend to perpetuate the genes which prompted it, by increasing the chances of survival in a closely related animal that carries those same genes. What is far harder to explain in these rational terms is the value of the extraordinary interest which elephants sometimes show in corpses even when they are decomposed.

After ten days of rotting in the woodlands Torone Sister Number Four was reduced to a foul black cavity enclosed by a bag of skin, with bones sticking out. The tips of her feet had been gnawed by hyaenas and some of the metacarpal foot bones were missing. I paid her a visit every day to watch the return of all the salts and minerals to the ground. In the rains this process was speedy and within a few more weeks I expected to see grass and herbs sprouting from the dark fibres that had once been her stomach contents.

On the tenth morning a large number of elephants came up from the south to the Ndala woodlands. I was curious to see what they would do if they found the corpse, so I parked the Land-Rover just behind the carcass, with a clear view, and awaited events. After a little while a large

matriarch named Clytemnestra appeared with her family unit close behind her. She was a fierce inhabitant of the south whose range overlapped in many places with that of the Torone sisters, and she must have known Torone Four when she was alive. As soon as she caught sight of my vehicle she brandished her ears and looked sideways in my direction. Having made this aggressive flourish she continued quietly on her path. Over the four years I had known her she had calmed down a great deal and was now almost used to quiet vehicles. The tourist explosion and the ever-increasing stream of cars through the Park even down in the wilder regions was gradually having its taming effect on all elephants except for the irreconcilable Torones and a few others. Clytemnestra continued for several paces, and then all of a sudden she caught a whiff of the corpse blowing towards her on the wind and spun round. Her trunk held out like a spear, her ears like two great shields, she strode purposefully towards the scent, like a mediaeval olfactory missile of very large proportions. Three other large cows came right behind her, heads suspiciously raised, until they closed around the corpse. Their trunks sniffed at first cautiously, then with growing confidence played up and down the shrunken body, touching and feeling each bared fragment of bone. The tusks excited special interest. Pieces were picked up, twiddled and tossed aside. All the while they were aware of my presence at ten paces' distance. Never had they come so close to me before. One of the young cows took two paces in my direction and tossed her head angrily; the others reacted to her mood, and the spell cast by the corpse was broken. They made perfunctory threat displays and moved away. But for my proximity I felt their investigation would have gone on longer, and I cursed myself for being too close.

Before this incident, I had heard of the elephant's graveyard, the place where elephants are supposed to die. This persistent myth I knew to be untrue after discovering elephant corpses scattered all over the Park. I had, of course, also heard that elephants took a special interest in the corpses of their own kind; it had sounded like a fairy tale and I had dismissed it from my mind. However, now

Iain and Oria Douglas-Hamilton photographed this group of elephants intensely examining the bones of a dead companion.

after seeing it with my own eyes I collected every reliable account I could find and the earliest I discovered came from David Sheldrick. In 1957 from Tsavo he wrote:

> There is now fairly convincing evidence that elephants have a strange habit of removing tusks from their dead comrades. In Tsavo East over the past eight years, the Warden has recovered a great number of tusks from elephants—which had died from arrow wounds or from natural causes—and has found in many instances that the tusks have been removed and carried anything up to half a mile from the carcass. In other cases, the tusks have been shattered against trees or rocks. Quite obviously, no hyena could manage to drag or move a tusk weighing up to 100 lb. for no purpose. The lack of teeth marks, and the fact that some of them are smashed, showed it could only be elephants that resorted to this practice.

Asiatic Elephants

In Asia the elephant has always been held in special reverence. Ganesha, the Hindu god of wisdom and prudence, has the head of an elephant. In various festivals throughout India elephants are richly caparisoned in embroidered finery studded with jewels and silver, and their faces are painted in a variety of designs and colors (opposite). King Bhumipol of Thailand was presented with a rare "white" bull as a trapping of power.

The Asiatic elephant comes from a different ancestral line and differs in important anatomical respects from its African counterpart. It is on the average about one third smaller and lighter, and whereas the African elephant is slightly swaybacked, the Asiatic is humpbacked. It has a high-domed forehead in contrast to the African's flat, sloping head. Its ears are triangular and only one third the size of the African's. Its trunk is smoother and has only one lip at the tip compared to the African's two.

Partly because of its fearsome aspect, the elephant was long used in Asia in warfare. In the fourth century B.C. Alexander the Great defeated elephant-borne legions in his conquest of northwest India. And as recently as 1862 King Mongkut of Siam (today Thailand) offered to send several of his best fighting elephants to President Abraham Lincoln for use against the Confederacy during the American Civil War. Lincoln politely declined—a good decision, for, even before the introduction of gunpowder, elephants had proved unreliable in battle except as intimidators. They were skittish, easily alarmed by unfamiliar sounds and inclined to break ranks.

In Asia elephants are still captured and trained for heavy work, a practice that dates back more than 5,500 years. Today thousands of elephants are used in many parts of Asia to carry heavy burdens, and they are a vital part of the lumber industry in Thailand, Laos and Burma, where valuable hardwoods such as teak grow deep in lush tropical forests. The burly elephant bulldozes its own roads through the dense underbrush and then easily maneuvers heavy logs along these lanes with its head and tusks. In mountainous terrain it is a surprisingly good climber, moving slowly and carefully, with a better sense of equilibrium than a horse. Work elephants are roused at dawn and given a leisurely breakfast and bath before beginning their tasks.

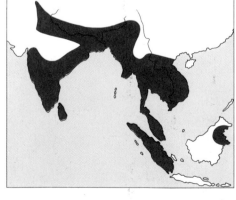

Like men, they take a four-hour rest when the equatorial sun is at its highest and hottest. Although elephants are excellent swimmers, they prefer to walk through shallow waterways. When they are in deeper water they hold their trunks above the surface, breathing through them like snorkeling devices.

Work elephants are still usually born in the wild; breeding them in captivity is too expensive. The gestation period of an elephant is 22 months, during the latter part of which the female can do no work and yet must be fed an average of 500 pounds of food a day. After giving birth she must devote a good part of the next three years to nursing her calf, which will not be able to begin its training as a work animal until it is 10 years old. Thus it has long made sense to capture grown elephants for training. This is done by means of the *keddah*, or drive. Trainers round up wild herds, from which they select the sturdiest young elephants, preferably females. Those over 30 are released as too difficult to train. Before a wild elephant can be trained, its spirit must be broken, and this is done in a seemingly brutal fashion: The beast is tethered with stout ropes and kept semistarved until it is too weak to resist when a *mahout*, or trainer, begins teaching it to obey commands. The fully trained elephant knows about 30 commands and displays a touching diligence in its effort to please its trainer, on whom it is now entirely dependent for food.

Like its African cousin, the Asiatic elephant is gradually losing its natural ranges to man's inexorable expansion. Forests are disappearing all over Asia as more and more land comes under cultivation. Sri Lanka, the island nation formerly known as Ceylon, had about 40,000 elephants four centuries ago. During the 19th century British and Dutch colonialists began clearing dense jungles and slaughtering elephants to cultivate the world-famous Ceylonese tea. Today, although Ceylonese elephants are legally protected, there are fewer than 3,000 left, more than half of them living in the wild on ranges that may be in jeopardy. Within a short time perhaps the only elephants left will be in captivity—anachronistic reminders of a gentle animal that was simply too big for the modern world.

Asiatic elephants inhabit the forests of India and Southeast Asia, including a small area of the island of Borneo.

Living Art Forms

These life-sized elephants (opposite) were carved from solid rock in 600–750 A.D. They are part of a monumental frieze at Mahabalipuram, India, showing animals, men and gods offering thanks to the god Shiva for the Ganges River. Ever since the Stone Age, when primitive artists engraved them on walls of caves, elephants have been a favorite subject with artists. Elephant sculpture, either religious or simply decorative, has flourished in Asia especially; it appears on temples and public buildings or as mosaics on walls of houses and fortresses. Even standing quietly, sleek and wet after a mudbath (above), elephants tend to look like sculptures. Or merely fording a river in Nepal (next page), carrying their trainers and their own dinners, their massive, purposeful grace is living art.

Shooting an Elephant

by George Orwell

George Orwell, the author of 1984 *and* Animal Farm*, was born in India and, after an English education, returned to serve with the Indian Imperial Police in Burma. In this essay Orwell tells of having to kill a tame elephant for "political" reasons. The fact that he hates what he does and despises himself for doing it makes the event even more appalling.*

In Moulmein, in lower Burma, I was hated by large numbers of people—the only time in my life that I have been important enough for this to happen to me. I was sub-divisional police officer of the town, and in an aimless,

petty kind of way anti-European feeling was very bitter. No one had the guts to raise a riot, but if a European woman went through the bazaars alone somebody would probably spit betel juice over her dress. As a police officer I was an obvious target and was baited whenever it seemed safe to do so. When a nimble Burman tripped me up on the football field and the referee (another Burman) looked the other way, the crowd yelled with hideous laughter. This happened more than once. In the end the sneering yellow faces of young men that met me everywhere, the insults hooted after me when I was at a safe distance, got badly on my nerves. The young Buddhist priests were the worst of all. There were several thousands of them in the town and none of them seemed to have anything to do except stand on street corners and jeer at Europeans.

All this was perplexing and upsetting. For at that time I had already made up my mind that imperialism was an evil thing and the sooner I chucked up my job and got out of it the better. Theoretically—and secretly, of course—I was all for the Burmese and all against their oppressors, the British. As for the job I was doing, I hated it more bitterly than I can perhaps make clear. In a job like that you see the dirty work of Empire at close quarters. The wretched prisoners huddling in the stinking cages of the lock-ups, the grey, cowed faces of the long-term convicts, the scarred buttocks of the men who had been flogged with bamboos—all these oppressed me with an intolerable sense of guilt. But I could get nothing into perspective. I was young and ill-educated and I had had to think out my problems in the utter silence that is imposed on every Englishman in the East. I did not even know that the British Empire is dying, still less did I know that it is a great deal better than the younger empires that are going to supplant it. All I knew was that I was stuck between my hatred of the empire I served and my rage against the evil-spirited little beasts who tried to make my job impossible. With one part of my mind I thought of the British

Raj as an unbreakable tyranny, as something clamped down, in *saecula saeculorum*, upon the will of prostrate people; with another part I thought that the greatest joy in the world would be to drive a bayonet into a Buddhist priest's guts. Feelings like these are the normal by-products of imperialism; ask any Anglo-Indian official, if you can catch him off duty.

One day something happened which in a roundabout way was enlightening. It was a tiny incident in itself, but it gave me a better glimpse than I had had before of the real nature of imperialism—the real motives for which despotic governments act. Early one morning the sub-inspector at a police station the other end of the town rang me up on the 'phone and said that an elephant was ravaging the bazaar. Would I please come and do something about it? I did not know what I could do, but I wanted to see what was happening and I got on to a pony and started out. I took my rifle, an old .44 Winchester and much too small to kill an elephant, but I thought the noise might be useful *in terrorem*. Various Burmans stopped me on the way and told me about the elephant's doings. It was not, of course, a wild elephant, but a tame one which had gone "must." It had been chained up, as tame elephants always are when their attack of "must" is due, but on the previous night it had broken its chain and escaped. Its mahout, the only person who could manage it when it was in that state, had set out in pursuit, but had taken the wrong direction and was now twelve hours' journey away, and in the morning the elephant had suddenly reappeared in the town. The Burmese population had no weapons and were quite helpless against it. It had already destroyed somebody's bamboo hut, killed a cow and raided some fruit-stalls and devoured the stock; also it had met the municipal rubbish van and, when the driver jumped out and took to his heels, had turned the van over and inflicted violences upon it.

The Burmese sub-inspector and some Indian constables were waiting for me in the quarter where the elephant had been seen. It was a very poor quarter, a labyrinth of squalid bamboo huts, thatched with palm-leaf, winding all over a steep hillside. I remember that it was a cloudy, stuffy morning at the beginning of the rains. We began questioning the people as to where the elephant had gone and, as usual, failed to get any definite information. That is invariably the case in the East; a story always sounds clear enough at a distance, but the nearer you get to the scene of events the vaguer it becomes. Some of the people said that the elephant had gone in one direction, some said that he had gone in another, some professed not even to have heard of any elephant. I had almost made up my mind that the whole story was a pack of lies, when we heard yells a little distance away. There was a loud, scandalized cry of "Go away, child! Go away this instant!" and an old woman with a switch in her hand came round the corner of a hut, violently shooing away a crowd of naked children. Some more women followed, clicking their tongues and exclaiming; evidently there was something that the children ought not to have seen. I rounded the hut and saw a man's dead body sprawling in the mud. He was an Indian, a black Dravidian coolie, almost naked, and he could not have been dead many minutes. The people said that the elephant had come suddenly upon him round the corner of the hut, caught him with its trunk, put its foot on his back and ground him into the earth. This was the rainy season and the ground was soft, and his face had scored a trench a foot deep and a couple of yards long. He was lying on his belly with arms crucified and head sharply twisted to one side. His face was coated with mud, the eyes wide open, the teeth bared and grinning with an expression of unendurable agony. (Never tell me, by the way, that the dead look peaceful. Most of the corpses I have seen looked devilish.) The friction of the great beast's foot had stripped the skin from his back as neatly as one skins a rabbit. As soon as I saw the dead man I sent an orderly to a friend's house nearby to borrow an elephant rifle. I had already sent back the pony, not wanting it to go mad with fright and throw me if it smelt the elephant.

The orderly came back in a few minutes with a rifle and five cartridges, and meanwhile some Burmans had arrived and told us that the elephant was in the paddy fields below, only a few hundred yards away. As I started forward practically the whole population of the quarter flocked out of the houses and followed me. They had seen the rifle and

57

were all shouting excitedly that I was going to shoot the elephant. They had not shown much interest in the elephant when he was merely ravaging their homes, but it was different now that he was going to be shot. It was a bit of fun to them, as it would be to an English crowd; besides they wanted the meat. It made me vaguely uneasy. I had no intention of shooting the elephant—I had merely sent

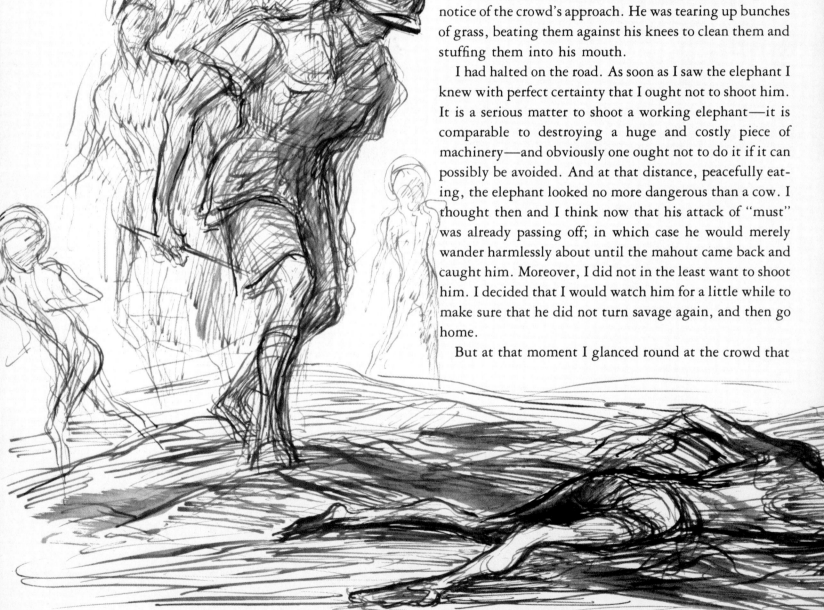

for the rifle to defend myself if necessary—and it is always unnerving to have a crowd following you. I marched down the hill, looking and feeling a fool, with the rifle over my shoulder and an ever-growing army of people jostling at my heels. At the bottom, when you got away from the huts, there was a metalled road and beyond that a miry waste of paddy fields a thousand yards across, not yet ploughed but soggy from the first rains and dotted with coarse grass. The elephant was standing eight yards from the road, his left side towards us. He took not the slightest notice of the crowd's approach. He was tearing up bunches of grass, beating them against his knees to clean them and stuffing them into his mouth.

I had halted on the road. As soon as I saw the elephant I knew with perfect certainty that I ought not to shoot him. It is a serious matter to shoot a working elephant—it is comparable to destroying a huge and costly piece of machinery—and obviously one ought not to do it if it can possibly be avoided. And at that distance, peacefully eating, the elephant looked no more dangerous than a cow. I thought then and I think now that his attack of "must" was already passing off; in which case he would merely wander harmlessly about until the mahout came back and caught him. Moreover, I did not in the least want to shoot him. I decided that I would watch him for a little while to make sure that he did not turn savage again, and then go home.

But at that moment I glanced round at the crowd that

had followed me. It was an immense crowd, two thousand at the least and growing every minute. It blocked the road for a long distance on either side. I looked at the sea of yellow faces above the garish clothes—faces all happy and excited over this bit of fun, all certain that the elephant was going to be shot. They were watching me as they would watch a conjurer about to perform a trick. They did not like me, but with the magical rifle in my hands I was momentarily worth watching. And suddenly I realized that I should have to shoot the elephant after all. The people expected it of me and I had got to do it; I could feel their two thousand wills pressing me forward, irresistibly. And it was at this moment, as I stood there with the rifle in my hands, that I first grasped the hollowness, the futility of the white man's dominion in the East. Here was I, the white man with his gun, standing in front of the unarmed native crowd—seemingly the leading actor of the piece; but in reality I was only an absurd puppet pushed to and fro by the will of those yellow faces behind. I perceived in this moment that when the white man turns tyrant it is his own freedom that he destroys. He becomes a sort of hollow, posing dummy, the conventionalized figure of a sahib. For it is the condition of his rule that he shall spend his life in trying to impress the "natives," and so in every crisis he has got to do what the "natives" expect of him. He wears a mask, and his face grows to fit it. I had got to shoot the elephant. I had committed myself to doing it when I sent for the rifle. A sahib has got to act like a sahib; he has

got to appear resolute, to know his own mind and do definite things. To come all that way, rifle in hand, with two thousand people marching at my heels, and then to trail feebly away, having done nothing—no, that was impossible. The crowd would laugh at me. And my whole life, every white man's life in the East, was one long struggle not to be laughed at.

But I did not want to shoot the elephant. I watched him beating his bunch of grass against his knees, with that preoccupied grandmotherly air that elephants have. It seemed to me that it would be murder to shoot him. At that age I was not squeamish about killing animals, but I had never shot an elephant and never wanted to. (Somehow it always seems worse to kill a *large* animal.) Besides, there was the beast's owner to be considered. Alive, the elephant was worth at least a hundred pounds; dead, he would only be worth the value of his tusks, five pounds, possibly. But I had got to act quickly. I turned to some experienced-looking Burmans who had been there when we arrived, and asked them how the elephant had been behaving. They all said the same thing: he took no notice of you if you left him alone, but he might charge if you went too close to him.

It was perfectly clear to me what I ought to do. I ought to walk up to within, say, twenty-five yards of the elephant and test his behavior. If he charged, I could shoot; if he took no notice of me, it would be safe to leave him until the mahout came back. But also I knew that I was going to do no such thing. I was a poor shot with a rifle and the ground was soft mud into which one would sink at every step. If the elephant charged and I missed him, I should have about as much chance as a toad under a steam-roller. But even then I was not thinking particularly of my own skin, only of the watchful yellow faces behind. For at that moment, with the crowd watching me, I was not afraid in the ordinary sense, as I would have been if I had been alone. A white man mustn't be frightened in front of "natives"; and so, in general, he isn't frightened. The sole thought in my mind was that if anything went wrong those two thousand Burmans would see me pursued, caught, trampled on and reduced to a grinning corpse like

that Indian up the hill. And if that happened it was quite probable that some of them would laugh. That would never do. There was only one alternative. I shoved the cartridges into the magazine and lay down on the road to get a better aim.

The crowd grew very still, and a deep, low, happy sigh, as of people who see the theatre curtain go up at last, breathed from innumerable throats. They were going to have their bit of fun after all. The rifle was a beautiful German thing with cross-hair sights. I did not then know that in shooting an elephant one would shoot to cut an imaginary bar running from ear-hole to ear-hole. I ought, therefore, as the elephant was sideways on, to have aimed straight at his ear-hole; actually I aimed several inches in front of this, thinking the brain would be further forward.

When I pulled the trigger I did not hear the bang or feel the kick—one never does when a shot goes home—but I heard the devilish roar of glee that went up from the crowd. In that instant, in too short a time, one would have thought, even for the bullet to get there, a mysterious, terrible change had come over the elephant. He neither stirred nor fell, but every line of his body had altered. He looked suddenly stricken, shrunken, immensely old, as though the frightful impact of the bullet had paralysed him without knocking him down. At last, after what seemed a long time—it might have been five seconds, I dare say—he sagged flabbily to his knees. His mouth slobbered. An enormous senility seemed to have settled upon him. One could have imagined him thousands of years old. I fired again into the same spot. At the second shot he did not collapse but climbed with desperate slowness to his feet and stood weakly upright, with legs sagging and head drooping. I fired a third time. That was the shot that did for him. You could see the agony of it jolt his whole body and knock the last remnant of strength from his legs. But in falling he seemed for a moment to rise, for as his hind legs collapsed beneath him he seemed to tower upward like a huge rock toppling, his trunk reaching skywards like a tree. He trumpeted, for the first and only time. And then down he came, his belly towards me, with a crash that seemed to shake the ground even where I lay.

I got up. The Burmans were already racing past me across the mud. It was obvious that the elephant would never rise again, but he was not dead. He was breathing very rhythmically with long rattling gasps, his great mound of a side painfully rising and falling. His mouth was wide open—I could see far down into caverns of pale pink throat. I waited a long time for him to die, but his breathing did not weaken. Finally I fired my two remaining shots into the spot where I thought his heart must be. The thick blood welled out of him like red velvet, but still he did not die. His body did not even jerk when the shots hit him, the tortured breathing continued without a pause. He was dying, very slowly and in great agony, but in some world remote from me where not even a bullet could damage him further. I felt that I had got to put an end to that dreadful noise. It seemed dreadful to see the great beast lying there, powerless to move and yet powerless to die, and not even to be able to finish him. I sent back for my small rifle and poured shot after shot into his heart and down his throat. They seemed to make no impression. The tortured gasps continued as steadily as the ticking of a clock.

In the end I could not stand it any longer and went away. I heard later that it took him half an hour to die. Burmans were bringing dahs and baskets even before I left, and I was told they had stripped his body almost to the bones by the afternoon.

Afterwards, of course, there were endless discussions about the shooting of the elephant. The owner was furious, but he was only an Indian and could do nothing. Besides, legally I had done the right thing, for a mad elephant has to be killed, like a mad dog, if its owner fails to control it. Among the Europeans opinion was divided. The older men said I was right, the younger men said it was a damn shame to shoot an elephant for killing a coolie, because an elephant was worth more than any damn Coringhee coolie. And afterwards I was very glad that the coolie had been killed; it put me legally in the right and it gave me a sufficient pretext for shooting the elephant. I often wondered whether any of the others grasped that I had done it solely to avoid looking a fool.

Hippopotamuses

Among the land giants, the hippopotamus ranks second in weight only to the elephant. A full-grown male may be 15 feet long and, although only five feet high, weigh 8,000 pounds. He is almost as big around as he is long, with short, heavy legs and a massive head.

In the hippo's characteristic position—at rest in a stream or lake, often with only eyes, ears and nose showing—it seems the most lethargic of animals. The appearance is misleading, because the hippo can be one of the most active creatures of the wild: a good walker in or out of water, a relatively fast runner and a ferocious fighter. Although it usually performs such vital functions as sleeping and mating in the water, it satisfies its need for food mostly on land. After sundown the hippo assumes the terrestrial side of its amphibious nature, emerging from the protective water to go foraging. Exclusively herbivorous, the hippopotamus will roam over miles of grassland to crop the hundreds of pounds of grass it consumes every night.

In areas where human habitation encroaches on its natural habitat, the hippo can do serious damage to crops—and to man as well whenever it is crossed in its instinctive determination to return to water by dawn or is otherwise provoked. Some nature writers claim that hippos kill several hundred people a year in Africa, attacking both on land and, by upsetting boats and canoes, in water. There are reports of hippos biting humans in half or, sharklike, taking a leg off with one crunch of its huge jaws. Although it has been described as "a wantonly malicious beast," the best evidence suggests that it attacks humans only when wounded or in defense of territories where the human has unwittingly trespassed. Lions, leopards and crocodiles sometimes go after newborn hippos, but the adult hippo's only consistent natural enemy is man, who kills it for its tough skin and excellent meat. The hippopotamus once flourished all over Africa but is now largely confined to areas in the central, southern and eastern parts of the continent.

The hippo's social life is often accented by violence. Before mating, a lusty bull must often fight other male challengers. These battles are not merely ritualized encounters, as is the case with so many other mammals, but deadly serious struggles. A fight between two well-matched opponents may last up to two hours, and a frighten-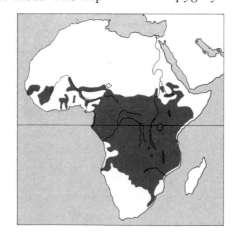ing spectacle it is (see pages 72–74).

A hippo has impressive dental equipment for fighting. Large incisors line both jaws, while the huge lower canines may reach a length of up to two feet. It is these long, dagger-sharp tusks the hippo counts on in a fight. They can cause deep wounds and much loss of blood.

The bull hippo has another method of intimidating challengers and impressing the female object of his ardor: He defecates copiously and, simultaneously using his short, flat tail as a catapult, slings his feces about indiscriminately. In these contests, the winner is the one who produces the most excrement in the shortest length of time. This is admittedly a less deadly method of establishing dominance than severing an enemy's vital artery, but it makes for some messy exchanges. Adult males also fling their excrement to stake out territories, and their tails are so strong that the waste matter may cover many square yards or cloud large areas of water.

Once the fighting is over, copulation occurs, usually in the water. Often the cow is submerged, and she must occasionally thrust her nose out of the water to keep from drowning. Once impregnated, the female gestates for about eight months, staying with the herd of other females and juveniles of both sexes, numbering between 10 and 40 individuals. She goes off by herself to give birth to a single offspring, which weighs only about 100 pounds, compared to its mother's two or three tons.

Hippos are among the longest-lived land mammals (after man, apes and elephants), and at least one case has been recorded of a bull that reached the age of 50. Hippopotamuses mature sexually at between seven and nine years of age, which can mean a reproductive period spanning some four decades.

The pygmy hippopotamus, which was not discovered until relatively recently, belongs to a different genus. It is much smaller, averaging about 500 pounds in weight and five feet in length when fully grown. Pygmy hippos live in dense jungle areas of western Africa, and though they are very shy and difficult to study in the wild, they thrive in captivity and have reproduced successfully in a number of zoos in Europe and North America.

Hippos were once widespread over Africa, but hunting and habitat destruction have eliminated them from western coastal areas.

Hippopotamuses are gregarious animals, living in groups of as many as 30 members, made up mostly of juveniles of both sexes and adult females, with only a few adult males. The herd stays together in the local watering spot (left). A powerful male (below) considers his muddy plot, no matter how small, his own and will defend it staunchly against rivals.

An Aquatic Horse

Hippopotamus, which in Greek means "river horse," is an eminently suitable name for a relatively fast-moving mammal that leads an amphibious way of life. Most hippo herds spend the day almost completely submerged in the muddy waters of Africa's rivers, lakes and streams and do not emerge until the evening feeding time. When it is not too hot, however, some sun themselves on sandy riverbanks, their bodies covered with a thin reddish mucous called "blood sweat." This substance, secreted through the pores, protects the animals' skin from constant exposure to water and the tropical sun. Although hippos spend more than half their lives in the water, they are not skilled swimmers. They prefer slow-moving or stagnant bodies of water about five feet deep that cover their bodies but still permit them to bounce along the bottom.

67

Water Babies

When a female hippopotamus is ready to give birth, she separates from the herd and retreats to a place where she feels comfortable and secure—often the water. Babies are sometimes born underwater, and an infant hippo learns how to swim before it can walk. If born in the water, it must immediately surface for its first breath, and during its 12-month-long nursing period the baby has to dive underwater repeatedly in order to suckle. Hippos are able to close their narrow nostrils by means of valves and to press their ears close to their heads when they dive. Young animals are capable of staying underwater for about 20 seconds at a time, while mature hippos can remain submerged for as long as six minutes.

Hippo cows, devoted to their young, keep their babies close to their sides (above), always placing themselves between the youngsters and any possible danger. The presence of hippos in a river or stream is extremely beneficial to the water's life cycle. The tons of excrement they deposit in the water and along the banks are fodder for the plant and animal life on which fish, like the ones seen with the underwater hippo at left, feed. The fish, in turn, are a major food source for the local villagers.

Waterbirds, such as the long-legged hammerhead (above) and the cattle egret (right) are constant companions of hippos. Often the birds arrive early at a battle between hippos, and after the fray they help the injured by picking flies and other insects from their wounds, thus preventing the spread of infection.

Mutual Aid

Unlike juvenile hippopotamuses, which are vulnerable to attack by lions, leopards, crocodiles and even irascible old bull hippos, the adults are virtually without enemies, except for other hippos and man. When hippos do become disturbed or threatened, they invariably retreat to a watery hiding place. The ideal refuge is a lake or river covered with water plants or obscured by low-hanging branches of trees lining the banks. Because hippos' ears, noses and mouths are situated on top of their broad heads, hippos can remain almost unseen as they take a few quick breaths, look and listen for a foe and once again disappear beneath the water's surface. The hippopotamuses' presence in the water is sometimes betrayed only by waterfowl, often seen perched on their heads. From that vantage point the birds scoop up insects and small fish. In return, they act as housekeepers for their hosts, removing the insects that irritate the hippos' skin.

70

A hippo herd crosses an African river

Encounters with Animals

by Gerald Durrell

Gerald Durrell, the author of more than a dozen books about animals, describes a fight between old and young male hippos for the attention of a comely female in a West African jungle. His affectionate portrait gives a scientifically accurate picture of the courting habits of the hippopotamus.

When I was collecting animals in West Africa we once camped on the banks of a river in which lived a hippo herd of moderate size. They seemed a placid and happy group, and every time we went up or down the stream by canoe they would follow us a short distance, swimming nearer and nearer, wiggling their ears and occasionally snorting up clouds of spray, as they watched us with interest. As far as I could make out, the herd consisted of four females, a large elderly male and a young male. One of the females had a medium-sized baby with her which, though already large and fat, was still occasionally carried on her back. They seemed, as I say, a very happy family group. But one night, just as it was growing dark, they launched into a series of roars and brays which sounded like a choir of demented donkeys. These were interspersed with moments of silence broken only by a snort or a splash, but as it drew darker the noise became worse, until, eventually realizing I would be unlikely to get any sleep, I decided to go down and see what was happening. Taking a canoe, I paddled down to the curve of the river a couple of hundred yards away, where the brown water had carved a deep pool out of the bank and thrown up a great half-moon of glittering white sand. I knew the hippos liked to spend the day here, and it was from this direction that all the noise was coming. I knew something was wrong, for usually by this time each evening they had hauled their fat bodies out of the water and trekked along the bank to raid some unfortunate native's plantation, but here they were in the pool, long past the beginning of their feeding-time. I landed on the sandbank and walked along to a spot which gave me a good view. There was no reason for me to worry about noise: the terrible roars and bellows and splashes coming from the pool were quite sufficient to cover the scrunch of my footsteps.

At first I could see nothing but an occasional flash of white where the hippos' bodies thrashed in the water and churned it into foam, but presently the moon rose, and in its brilliant light I could see the females and the baby gathered at one end of the pool in a tight bunch, their heads gleaming above the surface of the water, their ears flicking to and fro. Now and again they would open their mouths and bray, rather in the manner of a Greek chorus. They were watching with interest both the old male and the young who were in the shallows at the centre of the pool. The water reached up only to their tummies, and their great barrel-shaped bodies and the rolls of fat under their chins gleamed as though they had been oiled. They were facing each other with lowered heads, snorting like a couple of steam-engines. Suddenly the young male lifted his great head, opened his mouth so that his teeth flashed in the moonlight, gave a prolonged and blood-curdling bray, and, just as he was finishing, the old male rushed at him with open mouth and the incredible speed for such a bulky animal. The young male, equally quick, twisted to one side. The old male splashed in a welter of foam like some misshapen battleship, and was now going so fast that he could not stop. As he passed, the young male, with a terrible sideways chop of his huge jaws, bit him in the shoulder. The old male swerved round and charged again, and just as he reached his opponent the moon went behind a cloud. When it came out again, they were standing as I had first seen them, facing each other with lowered heads, snorting.

73

I sat on that sandbank for two hours, watching these great roly-poly creatures churning up the water and sand as they duelled in the shallows. As far as I could see, the old male was getting the worst of it, and I felt sorry for him. Like some once-great pugilist who had now grown flabby and stiff, he seemed to be fighting a battle which he knew was already lost. The young male, lighter and more agile, seemed to dodge him every time, and his teeth always managed to find their mark in the shoulder or neck of the old male. In the background the females watched with semaphoring ears, occasionally breaking into a loud lugubrious chorus which may have been sorrow for the plight of the old male, or delight at the success of the young one, but was probably merely the excitement of watching the fight. Eventually, since the fight did not seem as if it would end for several more hours, I paddled home to the village and went to bed.

I awoke just as the horizon was paling into dawn, and the hippos were quiet. Apparently the fight was over. I hoped that the old male had won, but I very much doubted it. The answer was given to me later that morning by one of my hunters; the corpse of the old male, he said, was about two miles downstream, lying where the current of the river had carried it into the curving arms of a sandbank. I went down to examine it and was horrified at the havoc the young male's teeth had wrought on the massive body. The shoulders, the neck, the great dewlaps that hung under the chin, the flanks and the belly: all were ripped and tattered, and the shallows around the carcase were still tinged with blood. The entire village had accompanied me, for such an enormous windfall of meat was a red-letter day for them. They stood silent and interested while I examined the old male's carcase, and when I had finished and walked away they poured over it like ants, screaming and pushing with excitement, vigorously wielding their knives and machetes. It seemed to me, watching the huge hippo's carcase disintegrate under the pile of hungry humans, that it was a heavy price to pay for love.

74

Rhinoceroses

The rhino looks like a holdover from prehistoric times. For the past 60 million years, rhinos of one form or another have roamed the earth leisurely reproducing themselves, living to a ripe old age in peace with other creatures of the wild. One of the forms, Paraceratherium, was the largest land mammal ever known to exist—25 feet long and 18 feet high at the shoulder.

Today the magnificently ugly rhino is on the verge of extinction. Only five species of the dozens that once abounded in Europe, Asia, Africa and even North America survive today—three in Asia and two in Africa. "Survive" may be too optimistic a word, for outside of zoos and game preserves the rhinoceros is almost as dead as the dodo bird. The great Indian rhinoceros can be counted in the hundreds. The related Javan is even nearer to extinction, with a total of only 25 to 40 animals living in the Udjung Kulon Reserve in Java. The Sumatran rhino, which has the distinction of having been described by Marco Polo, now exists in such small numbers that animal researchers can hardly find enough specimens to make studies of their behavior in the wild.

The two African species have fared only a little better. The African black rhinoceros (opposite) still numbers in the thousands, but it is found mostly within the confines of game preserves. The square-lipped, or white, rhino, a gentle creature with an undeserved reputation for ferocity, has at times been declared extinct; but a northern subspecies has been discovered that reproduces well in protected game parks, and its numbers are reportedly increasing. (The black and white rhinoceroses are misnamed; both are slate-gray. The "white" designation presumably derived from the Dutch word wijde, meaning "wide.")

The most distinctive feature of the rhino is its horn. The Indian and Javan species have one horn, the Sumatran and the two African rhinos two—one behind the other. Composed of keratin, a chemical substance with the hardness and consistency of a cow's hoof, the horn can reach a length of 50 inches and is a superb defense weapon.

Ironically, it is because of its horn that the present-day rhino is having difficulty surviving against man. In the Middle Ages the mythical long-horned unicorn became inextricably linked in popular imagination with the non-mythical single-horned rhino, and the magical properties formerly attributed to the unicorn were transferred to the rhino. It was believed, for example, that the horn, used as a goblet, would give unmistakable evidence of the presence of poison and thus save its user from a painful death; ground up, it would assuage a variety of ailments, such as epilepsy and the plague, and ease the pain of childbirth. Most important were the claims made for it as an aphrodisiac. This was not a new idea, because long before the Europeans had confused the unicorn with the rhino, the ancient Chinese had developed faith in the rejuvenating properties of ingested rhino horn. Babylonians, Greeks and Romans had all used the horn as a treatment to improve sexual performance.

Although modern scientific studies have disproved the theory, the belief still prevails among millions of Asians. On Asian markets a single rhino horn can bring up to $2,000 (far more than an ordinary Asian laborer can earn in a year), and in game parks a close watch must be maintained against poachers.

Undisturbed, rhinos have a life-span of about 40 years, most of which is spent eating and sleeping. They feed throughout the evening, night and early morning and then go to sleep. They average about nine hours of sleep a day. Their range is generally restricted to an area where daily trips to water are possible. They have excellent hearing and a keen sense of smell. They seem to rely heavily on their noses to help them follow paths that they and other rhinos have established. But an adult black rhino is extremely nearsighted, which has undoubtedly added to its reputation for aggressiveness because it has developed the habit of charging first and investigating later. A two- to four-ton, eight- to 14-foot-long rhino at full gallop is highly impressive. (For an account of one man's experiences with a nearsighted black rhino, see pages 86–89.)

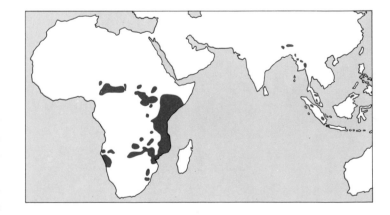

African rhinos are scattered over the south, central and eastern regions. Asiatic rhinos are in enclaves in India, Malaysia, Sumatra and Java.

A Lively Beginning

The gestation period for rhinos lasts for seven to eight months in the Sumatran (the smallest of the five species) and from 17 to over 18 months in the others. Newborn calves, like the three-day-old white rhino above, are on their feet just hours after they are born and follow their mothers wherever they go. The babies suckle at any opportunity, and though they begin eating greens when they are only one week old, they will continue to nurse for at least one year and possibly two. Young rhinos stay with their mothers until they are about three years old, but once a cow gives birth to a new calf (on the average of once every three years), she no longer tolerates the presence of an older offspring. The immature rhino reluctantly leaves its mother, sometimes attaching itself to another lonely exile or to an adult female but more often striking out on its own to begin the traditionally solitary rhino way of life.

When a rhino cow, like the African black rhino female at right, comes into heat she makes whistling noises to attract the bulls. If two males are present, rather than waiting for them to fight over her, more often she simply takes her pick. The chosen bull approaches the cow cautiously, for she often responds to his first advances by vigorously butting him with her horns. The bull may gallop away, but undaunted, will approach the cow again. This sometimes goes on for hours, during which the male tries—often unsuccessfully, as below—to mount the female. The two rhinos will sometimes face each other and gently rub horns before finally copulating, an act that can take as long as an hour. Once this lengthy encounter is over, however, the partners go off in different directions in apparent disinterest.

Deceptive Ferocity

Despite their awesome appearance, the rhinoceroses' horns are really the weak spot in the animals' otherwise formidable construction. The horns are made of dense layers of keratin, which makes them stiff. These great protuberances may unravel in places and resemble small tufts of hair. If force is applied, the horns can be ripped off entirely. When this happens only the slightest bleeding occurs and in time a new horn begins to grow. The rhinos' reputation for ferocity is rarely put to the test, since all other animals, including the usually fearless elephant, tend to avoid them. Rhinoceroses are basically solitary animals (except for the white rhino, which lives in social groups) and steer clear of others of their own kind. Fights between individuals are, therefore, rare events.

Of the five species of rhinoceroses, the African black rhino has a special reputation for its unpredictable and often nasty temperament. An encounter between two black rhinos (below and opposite) usually begins with a great deal of snorting and pawing of the ground. Finally the combatants lower their heads and with great speed and surprising agility rush toward each other. But when they get within striking distance rhinos will often stop dead in their tracks and retreat. Although serious fights entailing a locking of horns do occur, once the dominance of one of the competitors is established, the weaker one will usually retreat before either incurs severe wounds.

A Varied Family

Alike at first glance, the five species of rhinoceroses actually have marked differences. The Indian (opposite and below) has a skin covered by rivetlike bumps and divided into sections by deep folds across the rump and around the back, chest and neck. The distinguishing marks and relative sizes of the other species are shown at right. The rare Javan, like the Indian, has one horn and similar convolutions of the skin. The Javan's neck folds meet above the shoulder, while the Indian's end at the shoulder blade. The Sumatran has only the chest fold and, unlike the other Asian species, has two horns, one being a mere bump. The two African rhinos have folds on the sides of their necks plus two horns. The white has a distinct shoulder hump; the black does not.

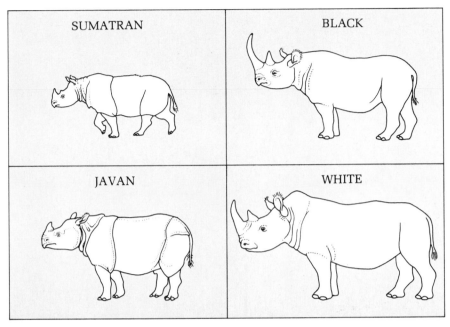

SUMATRAN · BLACK · JAVAN · WHITE

All species of rhinoceroses, like the African black rhino seen belly-up
(above) pass many hours of the day—and sometimes the night—
wallowing in the mud. The mud baths are essential for regulating the
rhinos' temperature and for keeping their skin in good condition.

In Africa, the wallows belong to all rhinos and are not defended, even during the dry season when the puddles are reduced to only a few inches of mud. The rhinos still manage to coat their entire bodies with the thick, protective slime by immersing one part at a time. The black rhino below gives its legs and belly a treatment while the mud on its head and back dries to a white dust.

ANIMAL KITABU by Jean-Pierre Hallet

Jean-Pierre Hallet, a Belgian naturalist, befriended a black rhino (which he named Kifaru, the Swahili word for rhino) in Uganda. Hallet describes how he managed to train the animal in this excerpt from his book Animal Kitabu.

Insatiably curious, the black rhino is at the same time extremely timid and equipped with only limited mentality. His hearing and his sense of smell are superb, but his vision is abysmally defective. Each of his tiny eyes, set on opposite sides of his bulky, elongated head, gives him a different picture to look at; each picture is tantalizing in its wide-angle perspective but horribly frustrating in its perpetual fuzziness. An animal Mr. McGoo, nearsighted Kifaru cannot tell a man from a tree at distances of more than thirty feet, cannot see any object distinctly if it is more than twenty or even fifteen feet away, and has to cock his head sideways to see, with one eye at a time, around the bulk of his muzzle and his massive front horn. Moving forward with the horn lowered, he is running blind.

By day as well as night, Kifaru hears and smells a whole world of fascinating objects which he cannot see. His curiosity drives him on to poke and probe among them—to look for the needle, as it were—but his timid disposition makes him fear, and fear deeply, the very objects that he wants to examine. He hesitates, agonized, while the two conflicting instincts boil within him. Usually he runs away but sometimes rushes forward to investigate with the world's most farcical display of bluff, noise, wasted energy, and sheer ineptitude—the notorious rhino "charge."

Once, near the Upemba National Park in Katanga, I watched a typically addlepated rhino stage a typically silly charge. He was busy with a big mouthful of twigs when he heard a frog start to croak about a hundred feet away. He stopped chewing, cocked his head, and listened—with leaves fluttering out of his mouth—then trotted anxiously toward the sound. As he approached, the frog croaked loudly and hopped by chance in his direction. A ton and a half of spooked rhinoceros made an abrupt U-turn, retreating to "safety." He sulked for a few minutes before advancing again. This time the frog jumped in the opposite direction, making him feel more confident: he lowered his horn and charged, smashing the frog under his hoofs without even knowing it. He returned to the spot, sniffing until he found it, and pawed at the little blob of pulp with a puzzled expression. . . .

Cursed with equally bad vision, the elephant acts with majestic calm and self-assured determination; his great intelligence enables him to solve the problems that confront him and to keep his warm emotions balanced sanely. Kifaru, commonly and mistakenly believed to be related to the elephant (if elephants could sue, they should sue for slander), behaves very like his real-life relative—the dim-witted, dim-sighted and hysterically skittish horse. . . .

"What the rhino really needs is a good psychoanalyst," I had long maintained to friends in Africa. "Somewhere, behind the bluff and bluster, the frustrations and neuroses, there's a good-natured animal who would like to make friends."

No one would believe it. Brainwashed by the hunters' propaganda, they looked upon Kifaru as a hardened criminal rather than a scatterbrained delinquent. Hoping to refute that point of view, late in 1959, I purchased a recently captured, full-grown black rhino from the Uganda Public Works Department, christened him Pierrot, turned him loose in a 250- by 200-foot kraal at my Mugwata game park, and walked into the kraal, determined to tame and train him.

Pierrot heard the gate close behind me, and stared nervously in my direction from his position some 150 feet away. He worried about the problem for several minutes before deciding on the traditional rhino answer—charge. Then he trotted toward me, accelerating, his head held horizontally. In that position his already poor vision was blocked by his front horn, so, as he launched himself into a

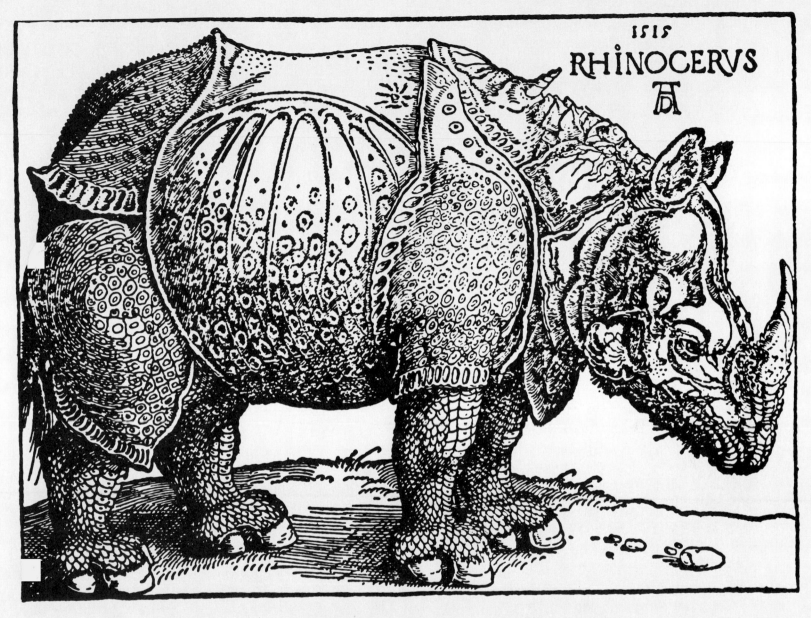

*This 1515 woodcut by Albrecht Dürer depicting the Indian rhino of King Emanuel I of Portugal
served as the model for many illustrations of the species until the end of the 18th century.*

furious gallop, he cocked his head to the side, straining to
see with a single eye. When he reached a point about thirty
feet away, where he could vaguely distinguish my shape,
he adjusted his angle, lowered his horn and thundered
toward me—a blind juggernaut committed to a fixed
direction.

I had about a second to answer or ignore him. If his aim

appeared to be dangerously accurate, I could make a quick
sideways jump like a rodeo clown; if not, I could stand my
tracks and watch his dust.

On this, his first try, Pierrot's aim looked a little too
good. I jumped. He shot past, snorting, with his tasseled
tail held high in the air. Decelerating to a stop more
than thirty feet beyond, he turned around and peered anx-

87

iously, trotting back and forth while he tried to find the target. . . .

This time I didn't have to move. Pierrot misjudged his angle badly, missing by a wide margin. His third attempt was even worse, and after five or six failures he stopped charging. Confused and obviously upset, he snorted, growled, shook his head and pawed at the ground. I let him sulk for ten minutes before I clued him to the target, jumping up and down and hooting like a baboon.

Pierrot raised his head, started to trot in my direction, spotted a small cassia tree at a ninety-degree angle, veered, galloped toward it under full steam, veered again, and wound up 150 feet to my left. He spent the next ten minutes trotting back and forth, head cocked, trying to find me. He was concentrating very hard, but he wasted his energy on two more small trees and a big clump of thorn bush. Then, when he finally spotted me, he charged, missed, charged again, and, of course, missed by an even wider margin.

Disgusted by the whole series of fiascos, a ton and a half of unhappy horned fury sat down on his haunches, grunting. As he did, I charged the rhino, yelling like a Masai. Appalled, he scrambled to his feet and stood, staring, until I got to within twenty feet of him. Then he fled in terror to the far end of the kraal. "The greatest bluffer in all Africa," as Carl Akeley once called him, had been shamelessly outbluffed.

We repeated those absurd maneuvers for the next four days, but I never charged the rhino again. Instead, I simply dodged or stood my ground as Pierrot continued to charge . . . and to miss . . . and to try again. If he became familiar with my appearance, I reasoned, he would be eager to satisfy his curiosity as soon as he decided that I wasn't going to hurt him.

The first signs of understanding came toward the end of the fourth day when I moved to a point within ten feet of the rhino's head and he neither charged nor retreated but watched quietly. After a moment, he started to worry again and backed off. Trying to reassure him, I made a noisy little retreat. That brought him back but he didn't charge: I was well within his field of clear vision and I was becoming a familiar if a somewhat baffling sight. Encouraged, I took a step toward the rhino. He took a step backward. So I took a step to the rear, and he moved forward one step.

We danced that little waltz, with minor variations, for a full month. It was dull work, especially so when compared to the quick, spectacular results that can be obtained with more intelligent animals. Working with my full-grown lion, Simba, in the backyard arena of my place at Kisenyi, I had tamed him in a couple of days and trained him, in *less* than a month, to sit, stand, lie down, roll over, mount a series of pedestals, and leap through a hoop of fire. Now, working with Pierrot, the pair of us simply stepped forward, backward, forward, and backward again. Friends and family had predicted my atrocious death beneath the rhino's hoofs, but the way things looked, I was more apt to die of boredom—either that or fallen arches.

The big breakthrough came, one day, as I was standing a couple of feet away from Pierrot's head. He suddenly turned his two-foot horn toward me, then rubbed his leathery cheek along my arm. I returned the gesture with a hearty slap on the neck, figuring that a rhino would, like an elephant, prefer a firm caress to an irritating little tickle. He nudged me in the ribs with his horn, rubbing it along my body. I took a dozen steps away from him, curious to see his reaction. He came toward me with an accelerating trot. I was in the direct line of charge but I stood my ground as the rhino advanced. He came to a halt with his horn less than two feet from my chest, then cocked his head and ogled me. . . .

Within a week, the horned fury and I were playing ball. We used a three-foot sphere of cattle hide stuffed with straw. I bowled it to Pierrot with my hand and he bowled it back with his horn. John Grindle's cricket-playing elephants would have laughed us off the field, but the rhino found it thrilling sport, smacking the ball enthusiastically but with very poor aim. His physical handicaps made it difficult to teach him more sophisticated games: he was too nearsighted, unable to jump or even to scramble over any kind of barrier, and he lacked grasping equipment comparable to an elephant's adroit trunk.

Tanzania's Ngorongoro crater: rhino country

Tapirs: Living Fossils

The only remnants of the once great rhinoceros family are the five species of rhinos seen on the previous pages and the family of tapirs shown above and opposite. Of the four species of tapirs, three live in the American tropics: the Brazilian, or lowland (above), the mountain and the Central American tapir. The fourth, the Malayan tapir, inhabits the forests of Indochina and the Malay states. The tapir has remained virtually unchanged for millions of years. It has poor eyesight and an acute sense of smell and prefers to live near water, which it uses for drinking, swimming and as a refuge from predators. Tapirs are vegetarians that feed on sprouts, leaves and branches, which they grasp with their short, fleshy trunks. They are shy, unsociable creatures that have been chased out of their ranges or hunted relentlessly for food and sport, rendering all species endangered animals.

Malayan tapirs (above) are distinguished by the blanket of white fur that covers the upper rear part of their otherwise blackish bodies. The mountain tapir (left) is the smallest of all the species and the only one that has a soft, woolly coat. All tapirs are accomplished swimmers and divers.

Giraffes

A human being finds it almost impossible to take in the giraffe at one glance. The human eye, starting out at the level of the animal's knees, must shift ever upward, up the stiltlike forelegs, past the thick chest, along the incredibly elongated neck until, straining, it finally focuses on the absurdly small head. At that distant height the sense of the animal's disproportion is reinforced. Although the giraffe's face is gently appealing, with long black eyelashes shading big brown eyes, its ears seem too large, and the whole towering structure is topped by two or more blunt, hornlike protuberances that give the creature an eternally surprised look. Having completed the survey, the viewer is reminded of Alice's words as she contemplated her own elongation in Wonderland: "Curiouser and curiouser."

It is as though there had been a mix-up in the evolutionary process, or as if two widely differing species had crossbred to produce an outlandish result. Indeed, the ancient Egyptians, who kept giraffes as early as 1500 B.C., believed them to be the offspring of a camel and a leopard, and the Romans gave them the name of *camelopardalis,* which still survives as the scientific term for the species.

The giraffe has elicited admiration from prehistoric times onward. Bushmen drew its unmistakable likeness on rocks. Arab potentates sent them to other rulers, as far away as China, as symbols of friendship and peace. In modern times the description by author Isak Dinesen in *Out of Africa* perhaps best captures the giraffe's gentle dignity: "I had time after time watched the progression across the plain of the giraffe, in their queer, inimitable, vegetative gracefulness, as if it were not a herd of animals but a family of rare, long-stemmed, speckled gigantic flowers slowly advancing."

The giraffe is the tallest animal in the world. A full-grown male can reach 18 to 20 feet and weigh in at one ton; the female is about two feet shorter and several hundred pounds lighter. But curious as its construction may seem, this gentle, cud-chewing herbivore is one of nature's triumphs, a marvel of natural adaptation to environment. Its habitat is practically all of the semiarid plain country of Africa south of the Sahara, and it is superbly equipped for survival there, even in the dry season when both water and ground-level forage become scarce. During this sere time the giraffe's long forelegs and endless neck enable it to feed on the leaves in the upper reaches of the acacia, its favorite food.

The giraffe is also endowed with acute hearing and keen eyesight. It can spot predators at a great distance, and its relatively short but powerful hind legs permit it to take off in a rush. In full flight the giraffe can sustain amazing speeds, sometimes running as fast as 40 miles an hour. This allows it easily to outdistance the lion, the only predator big enough and strong enough to try consistently to make a meal of it. But even the king of beasts will think twice before tackling an adult giraffe. For unless the lion can take it by surprise, which is hard to do, the lion can fall victim to the sharp and powerful hoofs that the giraffe uses to defend itself from attackers.

Courtship among giraffes is brief and sedate. The gestation period is 14 and one half months, and the female gives birth to a single six-foot-tall calf weighing between 100 and 150 pounds. The newborn comes into the world with a jolt, dropping about six feet to the ground, a fall that seems not to hurt it.

Giraffes long had a reputation for being mute, but dissection has revealed quite adequate vocal cords, and the animals have been heard to utter guttural bleats and grunts. Some naturalists think that because of their height and visual acuity they can see one another and transmit danger signals over great distances without vocal communication. There is another long-held belief about giraffes—that they do not sleep: They *do* doze intermittently on their feet, but they go into real sleep—lying down, with head resting on rump—for only very brief periods, averaging about five minutes at a time.

The giraffe has only one other natural enemy besides the lion: man. Thousands of giraffes have been killed in Africa for the tough leather the hide provides and for meat, which is palatable to native tribes. Since it does not compete with man or domestic cattle for food, the giraffe is spared wholesale slaughter. The uncertainty in the giraffe's future revolves around an issue vital to the survival of many other animals as well: the question of suitable habitat. The giraffe is safe as long as man gives it enough room.

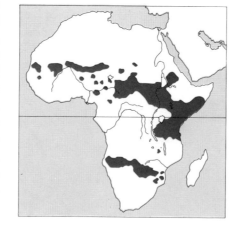

Giraffes are found in the savanna and woodland areas south of the Sahara.

Ungainly but Efficient

The giraffe has the same number of vertebrae in its neck as a man—seven—but in the giraffe they add up to the longest neck in the world, a distinction that turns out to be a mixed blessing. It enables the giraffe to feed in a leisurely manner and without competition on the tender shoots and leaves from the tallest trees of the savanna (opposite). But because its front legs are also very long, drinking (below) is a difficult chore. It requires a slow, awkward rearranging of all four limbs—a complicated maneuver during which a giraffe is vulnerable to attack by lions or other predators. When giraffes venture to a watering hole, they first look around cautiously and then drink copiously. In the dry season they get much of their moisture from the plants they eat.

The giraffe's tough, bristly, prehensile lips and long, narrow tongue are efficient eating tools. Working together, the tongue—which can extend 12 to 18 inches—and the lips can whip off the thorniest tidbits from a tall acacia with ease.

A herd of giraffes, whose netlike pattern of markings is called reticulated, pauses in its browsing among the acacias. The herds are so casual in their makeup that the members of a group are seldom the same for two days running. Bonds between calves seem to be stronger than bonds between adults. A giraffe "kindergarten," consisting entirely of calves, has been observed in the Serengeti. The females leave the calves on a hilltop every morning, returning to them only in the evening.

Necking and Rocking

Fighting to establish dominance goes on all year among male giraffes. They spar in a very special way, called "necking" (below). First, they line up side by side, usually facing the same direction. Then, moving around a great deal and using only their necks and stubby horns, they whack at each other until one of the combatants acknowledges the other's superiority by quietly withdrawing. The battle is usually more sound than fury. Although the blows can be heavy and can often be heard some distance away, real damage is seldom done.

A giraffe in motion has been likened to a ship pitching or a rocking horse rocking. Despite a minority report by one naturalist that it looks "lame in all four legs, besides having [its] shoulders dislocated," most observers find the giraffe exceedingly graceful. The rolling results from the peculiar giraffe structure and a gait called pacing, in which both left legs, then both right legs, move forward together. When a giraffe moves into a full gallop (above), its motion changes as both hind feet are swung ahead of and to the outside of both forefeet. Its slow rhythm is deceptive because a giraffe can reach a speed comparable to that of a horse, and some think the giraffe is faster.

An Odd Couple

The rare albino giraffe (right), sticking out like a sore white thumb, at least looks like a giraffe. The okapi (below), the only other member of the giraffe family, looks more like a donkey. In fact, "okapi" is the Pygmy word for donkey, and it was the Pygmies who first reported the animal's existence to Sir Henry Stanley during his exploration of the Congo in 1890. Although many okapis have since been captured for zoos, little is known about their habits in the wild, largely because they live in dense rain forests.

The Big Birds

Of the more than 9,000 living species of birds, almost all can fly. But some—ponderous giants whose wings have evolved into rudimentary or ornamental appendages—can't get off the ground. These flightless birds include the ostrich and some distant relations—the rhea, the emu and the cassowary.

The ostrich is the largest of all living birds. An adult male may top eight feet in height and weigh more than 300 pounds. Despite its bulk, an ostrich can attain a speed of 30 miles an hour and keep up that pace for half an hour. It is this running ability, combined with acute hearing and sight (its eyeballs are almost as big as tennis balls), that provides the ostrich with its best protection against predators—except for man.

Ostriches are social birds that travel in flocks of from 10 to 50. At mating time, the male chooses two to four hens, all of whom lay their eggs in a single shallow nest. Incubation is a cooperative task: The dominant female sits on the clutch by day, her dull plumage blending protectively with the surrounding countryside. The male takes over the job at night when his vivid black-and-white plumage is inconspicuous. After hatching, the chicks grow about a foot a month, and can look forward to a long life if they escape predators. In captivity, for instance, they have lived for as long as 50 years.

An ostrich when cornered can be an awesome foe, slashing at enemies with its unique two-toed, dangerously clawed feet. But ordinarily it would rather run than fight. Ostriches, especially when young, may try to evade danger by lying flat on the ground with their long necks stretched out, thus producing an almost imperceptible profile. This defensive maneuver has given rise to the persistent myth that the ostrich buries its head in the sand when frightened. It does not. Another old folk tale, one even mentioned by Shakespeare, does have some truth in it: The ostrich has the ability to digest metal. Ostriches will indeed swallow almost anything small and shiny. One in South Africa was found to have swallowed 53 diamonds. The gizzards of such omnivorous birds may come to resemble junkyards, but this odd habit has little ill effect because stones, which ostriches swallow soon after hatching to aid digestion, gradually grind down most foreign objects.

The rhea, often called the South American ostrich, bears only superficial physical resemblances to the ostrich. However, it is large—the largest bird in the Western Hemisphere, growing to five feet and weighing up to 90 pounds—it can run faster than a horse (and, more importantly, faster than its enemies), and it is just as curious as an ostrich about bright and shining objects.

The cassowary (opposite) and the emu are more closely related to each other than they are to the ostrich. Both are big, the adult emu at six feet being second in height only to the ostrich. Second in weight is the stocky 190-pound cassowary. It is distinguished by a big, bony helmet atop its head, and its plumage has a look of fur rather than feathers. It is pugnacious, dangerous, nasty tempered and a loner.

The emu, on the other hand, is usually friendly and curious when undisturbed. But its inquisitive ways have sometimes got it into trouble. In the 1930s, for example, the farmers of West Australia became so enraged at gatherings of emus trampling through their wheat fields that they demanded government action. A military expedition complete with machine guns was dispatched, thus initiating what was called the "Emu War." After a month of chasing the emus around the hinterlands, the soldiers returned to their barracks. Total casualties: 12 dead emus. The modern solution has been to fence off the vast wheat fields, leaving the big birds only a fraction of their former territory. Today only one species of emu is left, but it seems to be flourishing in the areas where it is allowed to run free.

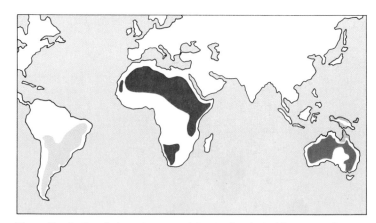

Rheas live in South America east of the Andes (light blue), ostriches in northern and southern Africa (red). Cassowaries (green) inhabit the forests of northern Australia, New Guinea and the nearby islands, while emus (purple) live in the semiarid plains of Australia.

Lethal Weapons

Even in repose the legs and feet of the cassowary look dangerous. Of its three toes, the two outer ones have strong nails, and the inner one bears a four-inch-long spikelike claw, adding up to a deadly weapon. In combat the cassowary leaps feet first at its foes in an attempt to disembowel them. Cornered birds have even been known to slash human beings fatally. Still, Papuans hunt them as game and tame young ones as pets. When they grow too big and ornery in captivity, they are either eaten or traded to animal dealers—one cassowary for eight pigs or one wife.

104

Birth Pains

The ostrich egg is the largest in nature, six to eight inches long and weighing more than three pounds. Getting out of it alive is no easy matter. The incubation process itself takes 40-odd days, during which time the eggs are prey to jackals, hyenas, vultures and humans. A few days before the hatching process begins, the chicks alert their brooding parents with chirps from within the eggs. Then, unaided, the chicks peck their way through shells as thick as china, an undertaking that may require hours and even days. Finally, they emerge, already a foot tall.

The Mating Game

Love among the ostriches is conducted according to an elegant, oddly graceful ritual, some highlights of which are seen in the filmstrip at right. The female begins the mating dance, stepping high and flapping her wings to entice the male (in the picture on the opposite page, the female is on the right). If the male is willing, he too begins to dance. Gradually the couple's movements become more precise and synchronized. If they do not achieve synchronization, the courtship is broken off. But if the couple is in harmony, the female sinks to the ground and mating takes place (below, the male is in the foreground), accompanied by a tremendous flapping of wings by both parties.

Were it not for ostrich farms, such as the one in South Africa shown here, the ostrich would probably be extinct. When ladies' fashions discovered the ostrich plume in the late 19th century, ostriches in the wild were slaughtered wholesale. To meet the increasing demand for feathers before World War I, ostrich farms mushroomed in South Africa, the United States, Australia and elsewhere. At the height of the feather craze one farm in South Africa alone kept 75,000 ostriches and shipped annually one million pounds of feathers valued at $15 million. Today the number of farms has dwindled, but ostriches still have some commercial use. Wing and tail feathers are plucked for hats and dusters; older birds are killed and their hides turned into handbags and wallets, their flesh cured into a dried meat. Since fashion no longer makes much use of their feathers, wild ostriches need contend only with hunters seeking meat and farmers who covet the semiarid ranges of the great birds.

Watchful Rhea Father

Like the ostrich, the male Common rhea (left) is polygamous, but he is even more possessive in his domestic role. He does all the talking—with a dull, booming sound; the hen never utters a peep. It is he who builds the nests, incubates the eggs and cares for the young. All that the females do is provide the eggs. The cock first gathers his harem of three to 12 hens, fighting off rivals who sometimes lure away those hens which still have more eggs to lay. If their new mates have not yet built their nests, these hens are forced to lay their eggs on the open ground.

After six weeks, the cock has a brood of chicks to worry about, and they follow him everywhere. He may wander a couple of miles a day, nibbling here and there at plants and gobbling up insects. The chicks do likewise. Ever alert and protective, the cock will attack anything that looks like a predator. He has even been observed charging small airplanes that were landing near his chicks.

Inevitably, some of the chicks go astray, and the lonely, plaintive call of lost rheas can be heard on late spring days echoing over the Argentine pampas.

Of the two species of rheas, Darwin's rhea (above), named after the English naturalist, is smaller than the Common rhea (left). Both species are in decline.

Flirtatious Mother Emu

Most of the time it is impossible to tell a male emu from a female: Their plumage is the same, and their heads and necks are equally bare. But at the onset of the breeding season the hen reveals herself—in a profusion of black feathers on her head and neck (above). She inflates her neck and emits dull rattling noises while the male emits a few noises of his own and grasps the skin of the hen's nape in his beak. Once the eggs are laid, it is solely the male's responsibility to incubate and raise the young—just as in the case of rheas and cassowaries.

Giant Reptiles

For many millions of years the giant reptiles dominated the earth. Today their descendants have dwindled to a relative few, and even these giants must still struggle to stay alive. For example, of the crocodilians (made up of three families—the crocodiles, the alligators and caimans, and the gharials), only 21 species survive; many more have become extinct. The largest species, the saltwater crocodile, grows to an average length of 14 feet. Of the numerous species of living lizards, only about half a dozen are giants exceeding six feet, and of these the largest—the Komodo dragon (opposite)—is confined to a handful of Indonesian islands that lie a few hundred miles east of Java. Some 200 species of turtles still exist, but the really huge varieties—the 500-pound tortoises—are now found only on the Galápagos Islands off Ecuador and a few islands in the Indian Ocean.

There are many reasons for the extinction of a species, but in the cases of the Galápagos tortoise and the crocodiles, man bears a major responsibility. From the early 17th century to the 1930s, pirates, whalers and hunters killed hundreds of thousands of Galápagos tortoises for their meat and oil. The lethargic animals provided a solution to the problem of fresh meat, since they could be kept alive on board ship a year or more with little trouble. (One old pirate wrote in 1697: "They are extraordinarily large and fat, and so sweet that no pullet eats more pleasantly.") Man's introduction onto the islands of his domestic-animal entourage helped wipe out more: Pigs devoured tortoise eggs; cats, dogs and rats ate hatchlings; goats, donkeys and cattle competed with the tortoise for food.

Today the Galápagos tortoises survive in large numbers only on two of the ten islands where once they flourished, but they at least seem to have a better future. In their native habitats they are protected by law, and they are being watched over and bred in captivity by the Charles Darwin Research Station, named for the British naturalist who studied the tortoises in 1835. (See pages 124–125 for his account.)

Man seems to have discovered a financial stake in keeping the tortoises alive: Thousands of tourists a year now take guided tours to the Galápagos Islands just to admire the unique giants. The tortoises' own long life-span (one captive lived to an estimated 177 years) seems also to be contributing to their survival; they are outlasting some of their enemies. Goats, for example, have been eliminated from some of the islands.

Crocodiles, too, have suffered at the hands of humans. Angry farmers have ruthlessly slaughtered the crocodiles, which will, given the opportunity, attack domestic animals. Though only a few species are actually man-eaters, their occasional attacks on careless humans have been recounted since ancient times. A zoologist reported recently that in his country, Sri Lanka, crocodiles have killed and eaten 53 people over a period of 25 years.

But crocodiles have suffered much more harm than they have meted out. They were so numerous at the beginning of the century in Tanzania (then German East Africa) that the government offered hunters a bounty for every skin. But the danger of the crocodiles' extinction arose with the demand for crocodile handbags, shoes and other items of fashion. Some governments, notably that of the United States, have passed protective legislation, but enforcement is generally poor, and poachers, who usually operate at night, are difficult to catch.

One giant reptile, the Komodo dragon, which reaches a length of 10 feet and a weight of about 150 pounds, seems to be in little danger from man. Indeed, almost since the huge lizard was first identified by scientists in 1912, on four of the Lesser Sunda Islands of Indonesia, it has enjoyed government protection.

If the Komodo dragon has an enemy, it could well be itself. The largest land carnivore on the islands, it dominates its empire without a competitor. The dragon lives partly on carrion but will also eat anything that moves—grasshoppers, rats, birds, goats, wild pigs, foals, deer, even water buffalo. A Komodo dragon in the act of devouring its prey is a terrifying sight. One 110-pound female was recently observed to dispose of a 90-pound wild hog in just 17 minutes. Its sharp, serrated teeth, razorlike claws and powerful limbs are highly efficient. The dragon attacks the huge, powerful water buffalo by darting in and severing an Achilles' tendon; then, while the animal is helpless, it quickly eviscerates it. And it even preys on its own kind— one reason perhaps why its population stays close to about 5,000.

Komodo dragons live on four islands in the Lesser Sunda group of the Indonesian archipelago.

Growing Up to Be a Dragon

When it hatches, a Komodo dragon is only 18 inches long. To avoid being eaten by adult dragons, it spends its first year in trees, living mostly on birds' eggs and small animals such as geckos, snakes and insects. Half-grown dragons occasionally climb trees, but mature adults are too heavy. Not until a dragon is a year old and about three feet long does it risk joining its elders on the ground. Dragons grow rapidly, reaching a length of six feet in their first few years. At that point of development their bodies and tails begin to take on their adult shape—wide, blocky head, relatively short, thick tail. Their tongues are long and deeply forked, like a snake's. Dragons have good noses and can pick up odors from carrion as far as five miles away. They do not move any faster than they have to, but they have been timed at 12.5 mph. They can swim, using their tails as a kind of propeller the way crocodilians do. To get at tethered goats, some dragons have been seen swimming through heavy currents to islets more than 1,000 feet away.

A large part of a dragon's day is spent doing nothing but sleeping and keeping cool. This torpor may be a reason for its longevity. Although no one knows for certain how long dragons live, some estimates go as high as 100 years.

114

The Komodo dragons on these pages are among the few living in captivity. The young ones below were hatched at an Indonesian zoo. As the lizards grow, their yellow spots will dissolve into the dull brown of the adult coat (left). Komodo eggs, which hatch in April and May, produce many more males than females—an odd phenomenon that may prevent overpopulation in an environment where food supplies are limited.

The Colossal Crocodiles

Crocodilians, the sole survivors of a primeval creature that also sired the dinosaurs, are the largest reptiles. Of three families—crocodiles, alligators and gharials—the biggest and most notorious man-eaters are the crocs. Using their awesome teeth to seize prey, the crocodiles devour their food either on land or in the water, raising their heads in the air before swallowing. Female crocodiles guarding their eggs are especially aggressive and will lunge after any intruder. Young crocs go into hiding for the first two or three years of their lives, until they are big enough to defend themselves against such predators as mongooses, hyenas and even adult crocodiles.

American crocodiles (above) have been hunted for their hides in such numbers that fewer than 500 now survive in protected areas in Florida, although there are other survivors in the Caribbean area. The Nile crocodile is another endangered species. The female at right gently cradles a newly hatched youngster in her mouth and carries it to the water where it will stay, protected by its parents, for six to eight weeks before going off on its own.

116

"Round about his teeth is terror," warns the Book of Job, and the saltwater crocodile, like the gaping youngster at left, is indeed a formidable creature. Saltwater crocodiles are the largest of the crocs, growing to a record length of 27 feet. They inhabit brackish and salt water and have been reported swimming 1,000 or more miles out into the Pacific and Indian oceans.

119

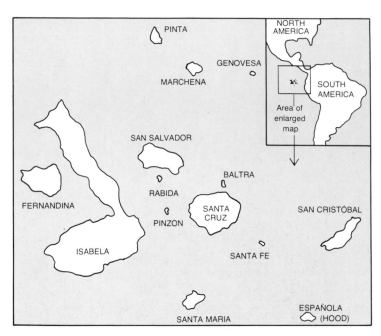

The Galápagos Islands (above), 600 miles off the coast of Ecuador, were discovered by the Spanish and named for the tortoises they found there. (The Spanish word for tortoise is galápago.) The volcanic islands were once the home of 15 species of tortoises, only 11 of which remain. Six species are being bred in captivity on Santa Cruz and then reintroduced to their native islands.

A Titanic Tortoise

The isolated habitats of the Galápagos tortoises and the absence of animals that prey upon them are elements which allowed these creatures to develop into the giants we know today. An adult male may weigh more than 500 pounds, and his prominently arched shell may be 50 inches long. A gentle herbivore, the Galápagos tortoise leads a very quiet, regular life. It moves slowly on its daytime rounds and usually beds down around 5:00 P.M. for 16 hours in a mudbath that helps insulate it against the 50-degree island night. During courtship the male becomes active and chases the female, nipping at her legs. The reluctant female responds by drawing in her legs, thus becoming immobilized. The male responds with a grunting roar, the only sound he is ever heard to make.

A Galápagos tortoise's head is proportionately small, its neck long. It cannot close its shell, but its forelegs—heavy, slightly flat and covered with large scales—help protect its retracted head. Its shell is susceptible to damage, but most shell wounds heal by themselves.

This rare tortoise from Hood Island in the Galápagos (there are only 13
adults left in the world) has a long neck and a flared upper shell. This
combination enables it to stretch higher for food than can tortoises
with dome-shaped shells who live on islands where vegetation
is more plentiful.

Two young tortoises ease their way among the adults (right) in the San Diego Zoo, which has been successful at hatching turtles in incubators. Giant tortoises lay only a relatively small number of eggs at a time—no more than 20—but a female may lay twice or more in one year. Below, a group of tortoises settles for the night, each one in its own spot, in the warmth of a shallow volcanic pond on Isabela Island. This part of the island, Volcán Alcedo, is estimated to support about 3,000 to 4,000 Galápagos tortoises—almost 40 percent of the remaining Galápagos Islands tortoise population.

THE VOYAGE OF THE BEAGLE

by Charles Darwin

This drawing shows Darwin measuring the speed of a tortoise in the Galápagos Islands.

During the five-year cruise of H.M.S. Beagle, *which set sail in 1831, the young naturalist Charles Darwin first made observations that were to develop into his theory of evolution. The ship spent a month in the Galápagos Archipelago, and in the following excerpt from* The Voyage of the Beagle *Darwin describes the giant tortoises he found there.*

I will first describe the habits of the tortoise (Testudo nigra formerly called Indica), which has been so frequently alluded to. These animals are found, I believe, on all the islands of the Archipelago; certainly on the greater number. They frequent in preference the high damp parts, but they likewise live in the lower and arid districts. I have already shown, from the numbers which have been caught in a single day, how very numerous they must be. Some grow to an immense size: Mr. Lawson, an Englishman, and vice-governor of the colony, told us that he had seen several so large, that it required six or eight men to lift them from the ground; and that some had afforded as much as two hundred pounds of meat. The old males are the largest, the females rarely growing to so great a size: the male can readily be distinguished from the female by the greater length of its tail. The tortoises which live on those islands where there is no water, or in the lower and arid parts of the others, feed chiefly on the succulent

cactus. Those which frequent the higher and damp regions, eat the leaves of various trees, a kind of berry (called guayavita) which is able and austere, and likewise a pale green filamentous lichen (Usnera plicata), that hangs in tresses from the boughs of the trees.

The tortoise is very fond of water, drinking large quantities, and wallowing in the mud. The larger islands alone possess springs, and these are always situated towards the central parts, and at a considerable height. The tortoises, therefore, which frequent the lower districts, when thirsty, are obliged to travel from a long distance. Hence broad and well-beaten paths branch off in every direction from the wells down to the sea-coast: and the Spaniards by following them up, first discovered the watering-places. When I landed at Chatham Island, I could not imagine what animal travelled so methodically along well-chosen tracks. Near the springs it was a curious spectacle to behold many of these huge creatures, one set eagerly travelling onwards with outstretched necks, and another set returning, after having drunk their fill. When the tortoise arrives at the spring, quite regardless of any spectator, he buries his head in the water above his eyes, and greedily swallows great mouthfuls, at the rate of about ten in a minute. The inhabitants say each animal stays three or four days in the neighbourhood of the water, and then returns to the lower country; but they differed respecting the frequency of these visits. The animal probably regulates them according to the nature of the food on which it has lived. It is, however, certain, that tortoises can subsist even on those islands, where there is no other water than what falls during a few rainy days in the year.

I believe it is well ascertained, that the bladder of the frog acts as a reservoir for the moisture necessary to its existence: such seems to be the case with the tortoise. For some time after a visit to the springs, their urinary bladders are distended with fluid, which is said gradually to decrease in volume, and to become less pure. The inhabitants, when walking in the lower district, and overcome with thirst, often take advantage of this circumstance, and drink the contents of the bladder if full: in one I saw killed, the fluid was quite limpid, and had only a very slightly bitter taste. The inhabitants, however, always first drink the water in the pericardium, which is described as being best.

The tortoises, when purposely moving towards any point, travel by night and day, and arrive at their journey's end much sooner than would be expected. The inhabitants, from observing marked individuals, consider that they travel a distance of about eight miles in two or three days. One large tortoise, which I watched, walked at the rate of sixty yards in ten minutes, that is 360 yards in the hour, or four miles a day,—allowing a little time for it to eat on the road. During the breeding season, when the male and female are together, the male utters a hoarse roar or bellowing, which, it is said, can be heard at the distance of more than a hundred yards. The female never uses her voice, and the male only at these times; so that when the people hear this noise, they know that the two are together. They were at this time (October) laying their eggs. The female, where the soil is sandy, deposits them together, and covers them up with sand; but where the ground is rocky she drops them indiscriminately in any hole: Mr. Bynoe found seven placed in a fissure. The egg is white and spherical; one which I measured was seven inches and three-eighths in circumference, and therefore larger than a hen's egg. The young tortoises, as soon as they are hatched, fall a prey in great numbers to the carrion-feeding buzzard. The old ones seem generally to die from accidents, as from falling down precipices: at least, several of the inhabitants told me, that they had never found one dead without some evident cause.

The inhabitants believe that these animals are absolutely deaf; certainly they do not overhear a person walking close behind them. I was always amused when overtaking one of these great monsters, as it was quietly pacing along, to see how suddenly, the instant I passed, it would draw in its head and legs, and uttering a deep hiss fall to the ground with a heavy sound, as if struck dead. I frequently got on their backs, and then giving a few raps on the hinder part of their shells, they would rise up and walk away;—but I found it very difficult to keep my balance. The flesh of this animal is largely employed, both fresh and salted; and a beautifully clear oil is prepared from the fat. When a tortoise is caught, the man makes a slit in the skin near its tail, so as to see inside its body, whether the fat under the dorsal plate is thick. If it is not, the animal is liberated; and it is said to recover soon from this strange operation. In order to secure the tortoises, it is not sufficient to turn them like turtle, for they are often able to get on their legs again.

There can be little doubt that this tortoise is an aboriginal inhabitant of the Galapagos; for it is found on all, or nearly all, the islands, even on some of the smaller ones where there is no water; had it been an imported species, this would hardly have been the case in a group which has been so little frequented. Moreover, the old Bucaniers found this tortoise in greater numbers even than at present: Wood and Rogers also, in 1708, say that it is the opinion of the Spaniards, that it is found nowhere else in this quarter of the world. It is now widely distributed; but it may be questioned whether it is in any other place an aboriginal. The bones of a tortoise at Mauritius, associated with those of the extinct Dodo, have generally been considered as belonging to this tortoise: if this had been so, undoubtedly it must have been there indigenous; but M. Bibron informs me that he believes that it was distinct, as the species now living there certainly is.

Credits

Bibliography

NOTE: Asterisk at the left means that a paperback volume is also listed in *Books in Print*.

Bere, R. M., *The African Elephant*. Golden Press, 1966.

Burden, W. Douglas, *Dragon Lizards of Komodo*. G. P. Putnam, 1927.

Burton, Maurice, ed., *The World Encyclopedia of Animals*. World Publishing, 1971.

Caras, Roger A., *Dangerous to Man*. Holt, Rinehart & Winston, 1975.

Carrington, Richard, *Elephants*. Basic Books, 1959.

Cott, Hugh B., *Looking at Animals*. Charles Scribner's Sons, 1975.

*De Camp, L. Sprague, *Elephant*. Pyramid Publications, 1964.

Denis, Armand, *On Safari*. E. P. Dutton, 1963.

Douglas-Hamilton, Iain and Oria, *Among the Elephants*. The Viking Press, 1975.

Durrell, Gerald, *A Bevy of Beasts*. Simon and Schuster, 1973.

The Editors of Time-Life Books, *Vanishing Species*. Time-Life Books, 1967.

Grzimek, Bernhard, *Among the Animals of Africa*. Stein and Day, 1970.

———, *Rhinos Belong to Everybody*. Hill and Wang, 1965.

———, *Grzimek's Animal Life Encyclopedia*, 6 Reptiles; 7 Birds I; 12 Mammals III. Van Nostrand Reinhold Company, 1975.

*Grzimek, Bernhard and Michael, *Serengeti Shall Not Die*. Hamish Hamilton, 1960.

Guggisberg, C. A. W., *Crocodiles*. Stackpole Books, 1972.

———, *Giraffes*. Golden Press, 1969.

Hoogerwert, A., *Udjung Kulon—The Land of the Last Javan Rhino*. E. J. Brill, 1970.

MacClintock, Dorcas, and Mochi, Ugo, *The Natural History of Giraffes*. Charles Scribner's Sons, 1973.

Milne, Lorus and Margery, and Russell, Franklin, *The Secret Life of Animals*. E. P. Dutton, 1975.

Moss, Cynthia, *Portraits in the Wild*. Houghton Mifflin, 1975.

Mountfort, Guy, *So Small a World*. Charles Scribner's Sons, 1974.

Neill, Wilfred T., *The Last of the Ruling Reptiles*. Columbia University Press, 1971.

Perry, Richard, *Life in Forest and Jungle*. Taplinger Publishing Company, 1976.

Peterson, Jack, *Animals of Africa*. Editions Minerva, 1972.

Sanderson, Ivan T., *The Dynasty of Abu*. Alfred A. Knopf, 1962.

———, *Ivan Sanderson's Book of Great Jungles*. Pocket Books, Inc., 1965.

Schumacher, Eugen, *The Last Paradises*. Doubleday, 1967.

Sikes, Sylvia, *The Natural History of Elephants*. American Elsevier Publishing Company, 1971.

Spinage, Clive A., *Book of the Giraffe*. William Collins Sons & Co., Ltd., 1968.

Willock, Colin, and The Editors of Time-Life Books, *Africa's Rift Valley*. Time-Life Books, 1975.

Zim, Herbert S., *Ostriches*. William Morrow & Co., Inc., 1958.

Index